Blessed Mother's Day
Michelle Reveé (Lasich)
Marcus Randall ~

. For all you are & have always been to
  your good Father & to me ~

. For your infinite love, commitment
  and pride in your incredible daughters
  ~ our cherished granddaughters ~
      Grace Layne Randall & Ginger Rose Randall
  to whom you & your good Jamie have
  give your hearts, minds, time & support.

            Love & shalom ~
            your grateful mother
            Mrs. William S. Lasich
            Vivian Esther (Layne) Lasich

The Book of
Mothers' Wisdom

The Book of Mothers' Wisdom

Love, Comfort, and Guidance from Mother to Child

Edited by Laurel B. Hoffman

CITADEL PRESS
Kensington Publishing Corp.
www.kensingtonbooks.com

CITADEL PRESS BOOKS are published by

Kensington Publishing Corp.
850 Third Avenue
New York, NY 10022

All Kensington titles, imprints, and distributed lines are available at special quantity discounts for bulk purchases for sales promotions, premiums, fund-raising, educational, or institutional use. Special book excerpts or customized printings can also be created to fit specific needs. For details, write or phone the office of the Kensington special sales manager: Kensington Publishing Corp., 850 Third Avenue, New York, NY 10022, attn: Special Sales Department, phone 1-800-221-2647.

CITADEL PRESS and the Citadel logo are Reg. U.S. Pat. & TM Off.

First printing (revised edition): March 2004

10   9   8   7   6   5   4   3   2   1

Printed in the United States of America

Library of Congress Control Number: 98005145

ISBN 0-8065-2562-2

Contents

Living   67

CONTENTS

Loving   161

Preface

As a certified social worker for the past eighteen years, I've long been fascinated by family life's enduring qualities. Despite the undeniable tensions that exist between parents and children, I'm convinced that this relationship anchors our most basic capacities to love, nurture, and befriend others. Without the experience of growing up with an interested adult caretaker, few of us would be able to form meaningful bonds with others.

To say this, of course, isn't meant to downplay the reality of loveless, "dysfunctional" homes; those families are far too common in today's society. But most of us, I believe, feel gratitude and nostalgia when remembering our childhood and teenage years. As we get older and, especially, grapple daily with child rearing, we often begin to appreciate more deeply the early guidance of our parents.

Certainly this has been true for me. My mother, who was reared in the 1930s and attended college after World War II, was a "super-mom" long before the term entered the English language. She briefly taught public school in Detroit before embarking on a business venture with my ailing father, Jerome. When he died of colitis at forty-two, my mother succeeded not only in developing the family business but also in raising three children on her own. My sister, brother, and I will always be grateful for the care and advice we received in those challenging years—and continue to receive today.

Besides my mother, three maternal figures in my life have been inspirational. Grandmother Anna's walk-up apartment always had an atmosphere of quiet contentment. When I was five or six years old I spent many weekends there and was treated royally. I especially remember taking long, leisurely baths while spicy fragrances from her native Russian cuisine filled the air. As I'd step out of the bathtub, Grandmother Anna would bundle me up tightly in a thick, fluffy towel, and I'd lie on the cozy bed until I was fully dry. She'd let me watch whatever television show I wanted and would sit near me as we shared fruit and candies. On those precious weekends Grandmother Anna made me feel loved and special.

Great-Aunt Gert ("Goo") was important in other ways. Born with neurological handicaps that affected her face and voice, she taught me tolerance and compassion—qualities that have helped me professionally as well as in my personal life. Despite vocal spasms, Goo was not shy. Because my mother worked late, Goo would unfailingly telephone every afternoon and talk with me about schoolwork, the importance of good grades, and my career aspirations.

By temperament Goo couldn't possibly keep phone conversations short, and it was unthinkable to hang up on her. As a result I learned to do many things while talking on the phone—including tidying our kitchen, scanning the newspapers, and copying my class notes. Later, when I had a high school summer internship at a psychiatric hospital, I would walk to Goo's house for lunch. Over toasted tuna-fish sandwiches we'd chat about my job, interests, and future goals. She was always encouraging.

My great-aunt Dorothy was certainly interested in my academic achievements but also wanted to hear about my friendships with girls—and boys. Readily offering advice, Aunt Dorothy helped me to develop social skills and graces. Well polished socially with lots of pizzazz, popular and active in many charitable organizations, she had a wide circle of friends. Aunt Dorothy was definitely inspiring to me. Her home was tastefully furnished and filled with attractive artwork, and she dressed sharply, too. Whatever aesthetic sensitivity I have I owe to my great-aunt Dorothy.

While my husband researched his recent *Book of Fathers' Wisdom* I became interested in producing a feminine counterpart or companion guide: What sorts of advice did historically famous women give their daughters and sons? How did they respond to their own children's problems, uncertainties, and questions about education, work, romance and intimacy, success, adversity, and faith? And could such guidance from the past still be relevant in our high-tech era?

As my research for this book progressed, I broadened my scope threefold: to encompass the interesting advice offered by women like Jane Austen and Elizabeth Cody Stanton to nieces, nephews, and others; to present lively anecdotes, not just private letters; and to feature the early guidance of mothers, grandmothers, and female caretakers to those who have subsequently become famous in our time. These include writers such as Maya Angelou and Margaret Mitchell, business heads such as Bill Gates and Katharine Graham, entertainers such as Lauren Bacall and Whoopi Goldberg, and political figures such as Hillary Rodham Clinton, Margaret Thatcher, and George Bush.

The task has been most enjoyable. It's difficult to describe adequately my excitement and pleasure in uncovering these gems of maternal wisdom and example selected from literally hundreds of biographies and autobiographies, memoirs, and collected letters. But as I completed my adventurous roam through history, four insights seemed key.

First, it's probably impossible to predict what grown children will most remember or treasure about their mothers. Many of the heartfelt reminiscences I found were not especially momentous in themselves, yet interestingly epitomized parental devotion to or wisdom for their offspring—whether such qualities shone through art, music, teaching, or even humor. In a way this suggests that every moment between mothers and their children has a wonderful potential for long-lasting meaning.

Second, our words of advice can have real impact. Perhaps it has always seemed to parents that their youngsters turn the proverbial deaf ear to their guidance, but after closely examining the lives of so many influential people I'm now sure that something deep does get through. We should never underestimate the influence our advice has.

Third, the really important things in life—love, livelihood, and health—have remained essentially the same over the centuries. Outer circumstances certainly change, but the human heart doesn't. Thus the sentiments expressed in these wide-ranging letters and memoirs about personal triumphs and disappointments are as relevant as this afternoon's phone call home, or to a distant college dorm.

And finally, I'm more convinced than ever that of all human ties, the bond between mothers and children is perhaps the world's most beautiful. We can't always articulate our feelings about this relationship, but I'm grateful that the writers here were able to do so with such enduring power. As Abigail Alcott wrote to her sleeping daughter Louisa May, "Your little note gave me so much delight that I cannot close my eyes without first thanking you and blessing God who gave you this tender love for your mother. . . . I shall lay this on your pillow, put a warm kiss on your lips, and say a little prayer over you."

Or, nearly a century later, as Grace Hemingway reminded her restless twenty-one-year-old son Ernest, "Your mother is waiting to welcome you, whether it is in this world or the next, loving you and longing for your love."

It's hard to be clearer than that. In a time when motherhood is faced with many new challenges and forms of expression, I hope that these varied selections—certainly not intended as definitive or exhaustive—will help to prove that mothers' love and wisdom are enduring and important.

Acknowledgments

This book would scarcely have been possible without the valuable help of many people. The enthusiasm of my literary agent, Alice Fried Martell, was instrumental in bringing this project to the attention of editor Hillel Black, whose literary judgment, good cheer, and patience have been much appreciated. Working with editor Monica Harris has likewise been a delight. For their conceptual contributions, I'm much indebted to my brother, David; my sister, Eleanor; and my sister-in-law Jackie. As a former teacher, my mother offered a variety of helpful suggestions from the outset. My children's many teachers have also inspired me by providing insights about coping with youngsters' everyday problems and challenges.

On the home front, I wish to thank three individuals for their boundless encouragement. My children, Aaron and Jeremy, by insisting often that I take a break, helped me to stay cheerful and balanced—and to put "motherly wisdom" into challenging daily practice. My husband, Edward, more than any other person, gave me the emotional support to complete the project and fulfill my own expectations for it.

Learning

Mary Caldicott and her daughter Helen

―――――

On Becoming Politically Astute

Australian Helen Caldicott trained as a physician and devoted herself to the treatment of children afflicted with cystic fibrosis—but it was in the political turmoil of the 1970s and 1980s that she found her true calling. Resigning from the Harvard Medical School faculty, Helen helped to found and served as the first president of Physicians for Social Responsibility (PSR) and Women's Action for Nuclear Disarmament (WAND), two organizations at the forefront of the nuclear-freeze movement. Over the next decade, Caldicott brought her message to world leaders, to the media, and to audiences of thousands, whom she roused with unique elegance. In 1985 PSR's umbrella affiliate, the International Physicians for the Prevention of Nuclear War, was the recipient of the Nobel Peace Prize.

Caldicott remains a tireless advocate for peace and nuclear disarmament around the globe. Where did her moral passion originate? In her autobiography, *Desperate Passion,* the influential physician recalled:

Mum was one of the most intelligent women I ever knew. Her birthright was her inquiring mind and her hunger for information and knowledge. . . .

She was fascinated by politics and history; and she kept abreast with everything. My first memory of her finely tuned political instincts goes back to when I was four and standing in the kitchen and she suddenly announced: "Hitler has turned on Russia—thank God, we're saved." She was right. Hitler couldn't win the war by fighting on two fronts simultaneously. Her political intuition was unerring; her analyses of events were rarely those in the newspapers or radio, but in the long run, she was almost always right. . . . Forty years ago, she worried about the consequences of world overpopulation, and as early as 1960, she could see that computers would eventually put people out of work. Her perceptions were always sure, and from her, I inherited my political intuition.

Hannah Chaplin and her son Charlie

———•••••••———

On Spiritual Ideals

Born into a poor London family, Charlie Chaplin became one of the world's most famous movie actors and directors. He started as an eight-year-old vaudeville performer; his film stardom began in 1914, when he first appeared as the Tramp or the Little Fellow in *Kid Auto Races at Venice*. Looking undersized and undernourished, Chaplin sported a battered derby hat, ill-fitting clothes, and a bamboo cane and shuffled unsteadily as he walked—yet exuded an air of lilting confidence and readiness for adventure.

In such popular films as *City Lights, The Great Dictator* (which ridiculed Adolf Hitler), and *Modern Times,* Chaplin offered biting social criticism through humor. His role typically spoke to the plight of society's poor and outcast. In *My Autobiography,* Chaplin reminisced about his mother's influence on his humanitarian outlook:

I remember an evening. . . . I lay in bed recovering from a fever. . . . It was late afternoon, and [Mother] sat with her back to the window reading, acting and explaining in her inimitable way the New Testament and Christ's love and pity for the poor and for little children. Perhaps her emotion was due to my illness, but she gave me the most luminous and appealing interpretation of Christ that I had ever heard or seen. . . .

She read into the dusk, stopping only to light the lamp, then told of the faith that Jesus inspired in the sick, that they had only to touch the hem of His garments to be healed.

As [Mother] continued, tears welled up in her eyes. She. . . . had so carried me away that I wanted to die that very night and meet Jesus. But Mother was not so enthusiastic. "Jesus wants you to live first and fulfill your destiny here," she said. In that dark room in the basement at Oakley Street, Mother illuminated to me the kindliest light this world has ever known, which has endowed literature and the theatre with their greatest and richest themes: love, pity, and humanity.

Annie Henderson and her granddaughter Maya Angelou

———————

On Contentment

When Maya Angelou read her newest poem at President Bill Clinton's 1993 inauguration, it was another landmark achievement in her multifaceted career. The author of numerous magazine articles and more than ten books, including *I Know Why the Caged Bird Sings, I Shall Not Be Moved,* and *Now Sheba Sings the Song,* Angelou has earned both Pulitzer Prize and National Book Award nominations. Raised in segregated, rural Arkansas, she worked with Dr. Martin Luther King Jr. in the 1960s. Angelou has achieved acclaim as an actress, playwright, producer, and director and has made hundreds of television appearances. She also teaches American studies at Wake Forest University in North Carolina.

In her memoir, *Wouldn't Take Nothing for My Journey Now,* Angelou reminisced about her childhood:

When my grandmother was raising me in Stamps, Arkansas, she had a particular routine when people who were known to be whiners entered her store. Whenever she saw a known complainer coming, she would call me from whatever I was doing and say conspiratorially, "Sister, come inside, Come." Of course I would obey.

My grandmother would ask the customer, "How are you doing today, Brother Thomas?" And the person would reply, "Not so good." There would be a distinct whine in the voice. "Not so good today, Sister Henderson. You see, it's this summer. I just hate it. Oh, I hate it so much. It just frazzles me up and frazzles me down. I just hate the heat. It's almost killing me." Then my grandmother would stand stoically, her arms folded, and mumble, "Uh-huh, uh-huh." And she would cut her eyes at me to make certain that I heard the lamentation.

Another time a whiner would mewl, "I hate plowing. That packed-down dirt ain't got no reasoning, and mules ain't got good sense. . . . Sure ain't. It's killing me. I can't ever seem to get done. My feet and my hands stay sore, and I get dirt in my eyes and up my nose. I just can't stand it." And my grandmother, again stoically with her arms folded, would say "Uh-huh, uh-huh," and then look at me and nod.

As soon as the complainer was out of the store, my grandmother would call to me to stand in front of her. And then she would say the same thing she had said at least a thousand times, it seemed to me. "Sister, did you hear what Brother So-and-So or Sister Much to Do complained about? You heard that?" And I would nod. Mama would continue, "Sister, there are people who went to sleep all over the world last night, poor and rich and white and black, but they will never wake again. Sister, those who expected to rise did not, their beds became their cooling boards, and their blankets became their winding sheets. And those dead folks would give anything, anything at all for just five minutes of this weather or ten minutes of that plowing that person was grumbling about. So you watch yourself about complaining, Sister. What you're supposed to do when you don't like a thing is change it. If you can't change it, change the way you think about it. Don't complain."

It is said that persons have few teachable moments in their lives. Mamma seems to have caught me at each one I had between the age of three and thirteen. Whining is not only graceless, but can be dangerous. It can alert a brute that a victim is in the neighborhood.

Clarissa Miller and her daughter
Agatha Christie

●●●●●●

On Acceptance

Agatha Christie, born in Devon, England, in 1890, was acclaimed as one of the greatest mystery writers of our age. She was educated at home by her mother. While serving as a volunteer nurse during World War I she began actively writing and published her first novel soon after. With the appearance of *The Murder of Roger Ackroyd* in 1926, Agatha gained major recognition. There followed seventy-five successful novels, twenty-five of them featuring the detective Hercule Poirot. *Witness for the Prosecution, Death on the Nile,* and *Murder on the Orient Express* were all adapted for film.

In Christie's *An Autobiography,* the renowned author affectionately recalled her mother's guidance:

I think late Victorian parents were more realistic and had really more consideration for their children and for what would make a happy and successful life for them. There was much less keeping up with the Joneses. Nowadays I often feel that it is for one's *own* prestige that one wants one's children to succeed.

The Victorians looked dispassionately at their offspring and made up their minds about the capacities. A. was obviously going to be "the pretty one." B. was "the clever one." C. was going to be plain and was definitely *not* intellectual. Good works would be C.'s best chance. And so on. Sometimes, of course, they were wrong, but on the whole, it worked. There is an enormous relief in not being expected to produce something that you haven't got.

The general standpoint in my young days had a certain humility. You accepted what you were. You had assets and you had liabilities. Like a hand at cards, having been dealt it, you sorted out your cards and decided how best to play them. There was, I am almost sure, less envy and resentment of those more gifted or better off.

Mabel Russell and her daughter Brooke Astor

＊＊＊＊＊＊

On Conversation

Brooke Astor, one of New York City's most important civic figures and philanthropists, was born in Portsmouth, New Hampshire. She was largely self-educated and eventually found a career as a magazine journalist. Once divorced and twice widowed, she was married to— among others—the late Vincent Astor, who left Brooke in 1959 with a fortune that allowed her to become a major philanthropist. In this capacity the highly sociable Brooke has been a generous patron of the museums, landmark preservation projects, and cultural institutions, especially the New York Public Library, where she served as a trustee.

In her autobiography, *Footprints,* Brooke reminisced about her early upbringing:

> I learned early in life that one has to work constantly to keep a relationship going. One of the ways I was taught this was by conversation. Not just talking, but conversation, by which was meant

talk that had real meaning and flavor and would bind people together, that would help them exchange ideas, facts, viewpoints, problems, and laughter.

And where better than at the family dinner table? "Having a real meal together is like going to a market place," said Mother. "Each one of us should bring something to it." ... [Her] emphasis on talk forced me to think, to look about me, to find new interests, and to become interested in other people's ideas. "If you are not interested in what is going on, there is nothing to talk about."

It is not easy for a grown-up to make a child participate in a different world, but Mother made it easy. I was like Alice in Wonderland and even if things were "curiouser and curiouser" and I did not really understand them, they aroused my interest and stimulated me. It was a wonderful gift that Mother gave me, because I now find it impossible to be bored. Mother made a story out of everything. Because I was brought up to express myself, I feel that, given the chance, I can talk to, and get on with, almost anyone.

Hortense Carlisle and her daughter Kitty

••••••••

On Culture

Kitty Carlisle Hart, the actress and singer, has a long record of achievement in the arts and public service. Spanning six decades, her career has encompassed movies, Broadway theater, the Metropolitan Opera of New York, and, of course, such television shows as the long-running *To Tell the Truth*. Married to the late Pulitzer Prize–winning playwright-director Moss Hart, Kitty served from 1976–1996 as the chairperson of the New York State Council on the Arts. To honor such public service, the Kitty Carlisle Theater at the Empire State Plaza was dedicated to her.

In her autobiography, *Kitty*, the actress reminisced about her early life:

> My father died when I was ten years old. . . .
> After my father died, my mother's friends expected her to

sit . . . wait for another husband. [Instead] She sold the house, took my father's insurance money, tucked her violin under one arm, me under the other, and [left] . . .

What pushed my mother to Europe . . . ? I think the real reason was her ambition for me. She wanted to make me a suitable marriage, which in her terms meant well above my station. She was like the ladies in the Henry James stories who took their daughters to Europe to make brilliant marriages, except unlike them, we had no money and no entrée. But somewhere in the back of Mother's mind was the idea of grooming me for a rich prince or, failing that, a not-too-impoverished baron. She was very farsighted; I was only eleven years old. . . .

[In Paris] I had had a truly progressive education. I learned what I needed to know when I needed to know. I stopped formal school at fifteen, but I was tutored at home. I had lessons in everything: languages, elocution, history of art, and comparative religion. No one cared about college or degrees for girls in those days in Europe, but Mother believed in culture—for me.

When I complained I had nothing to do and no one to play with, Mother, who had her feet firmly planted under the bridge table, would say: "There's a museum on every corner in Paris; go to the Louvre or the Musée Grevin. Or go to a concert. Go to the Opera-Comique. Your mind is your house. Furnish it!"

Louisa Singer and her son Isaac

◆◆◆◆◆◆◆

On Good Over Evil

Isaac Bashevis Singer was born in Poland to an esteemed rabbi and an equally devout mother. He emigrated to the United States before World War II and slowly achieved fame as a writer. In 1978 Singer won the Nobel Prize for literature in recognition of his masterful short stories and novels. Among his best-known works are *Satan in Goray, The Magician of Lublin, Yentl,* and *The Spinoza of Market Street.* Writing in Yiddish, he created memorable characters who struggled with religious, moral, and sexual impulses to find meaning in human life. In his memoir, *A Little Boy in Search of God,* the novelist recalled this key childhood episode:

> We starved at home. Bitter frosts raged outside, but our stove wasn't lit. Mother lay in bed all day and read her books of morals—*Duty of the Heart, The Book of Punishment, The Good Heart,* and occasionally the *Book of the Convenant.* Her face was

white and bloodless. She, too, sought the answers to the eternal questions, but her faith remained firm. She didn't cast a speck of doubt upon the Almighty.

Mother argued with my older brother: "It isn't the Creator's fault. He wanted to give the Torah to Esau and Ishmael but they rejected it." My brother asked: "Were you there?" He denied the concept of free choice. There was no such thing as free will.

Mother grimaced at this blasphemy and said: "May the Almighty forgive your words."

"There is no Almighty. Man is an animal like all animals. This whole war is on account of oil."

This was the first time I had ever heard such words. Oil, of all things? All the time we had lived in number 10 we had used oil in our lamps. Now that we lived in number 12 we used gas. It seemed incredible to me that Germany, Russia, England, and France should fight over such a filthy thing as oil, but my brother soon explained it.

Mother heard him out and said: "They only need an excuse to fight. Today they fight over oil; tomorrow, it'll be over soap or cream of tartar. The fact is that they are evildoers and the evildoer must commit evil. All they need is an excuse."

Dorotea Chavez and her son Cesar

—●——●——●——●——●——

On Nonviolence

Cesar Chavez was the charismatic founder and leader of the United Farm Workers of America (UFWA), which he established in 1962 to improve conditions for migrant laborers on farms. The group captured the public eye when Chavez organized boycotts of supermarket produce such as lettuce and grapes. Largely because of his direction the UFWA won its first contracts in 1970.

Raised in rural Arizona by parents who were Mexican immigrants, Chavez knew poverty from firsthand experience. His family became migrant farm workers during the Great Depression, and he and his siblings attended more than thirty public schools while growing up. In his memoir, *Cesar Chavez, Autobiography of La Causa,* the influential labor organizer recalled:

> [My mom] was the sort of woman who had time for her children, who would talk with us. She used many *dichos*—proverbs—

and they all had a real purpose. "What you do to others, others do to you" was one of them. "He who holds the cow, sins as much as he who kills her."

She also gave us a lot of *consejos*—advice. She didn't wait until something went wrong, nor was she scolding when she was doing it. It was part of the training.

When I look back, I see her sermons had tremendous impact on me. I didn't know it was nonviolence then, but after reading Gandhi, St. Francis, and other exponents of nonviolence, I began to clarify that in my mind.

Despite a culture where you're not a man if you don't fight back, [Mom] would say, "No, it's best to turn the other cheek.

God gave you senses like eyes and mind and tongue, and you can get out of anything." She would say, "It takes two to fight." That was her favorite. "It takes two to fight, and one can't do it alone." She had all kinds of proverbs for that. "It's better to say that he ran from here than to say he died here."

"When I was young, I didn't realize the wisdom in her words," Chavez remarked late in life, "but it has been proved to me so many times since. Today I appreciate the advice, and I use quite a few of the *dichos,* especially in Spanish."

Julia Davis and her grandson Bayard Rustin

●●●●●●

On Conflict

Bayard Rustin was one of the most complex and interesting figures of the civil rights movement. He is perhaps best known as the organizer of the historic 1963 march on Washington, D.C., where Dr. Martin Luther King Jr. delivered his memorable "I Have a Dream" oration. Rustin not only helped to organize the Montgomery bus boycott of 1955–1956 but also drew up the original plan for the Southern Christian Leadership Council, the organization that spearheaded Dr. King's nonviolent crusade.

As executive director from 1964 to 1987 of the A. Phillip Randolph Institute, Rustin was deeply committed to the Gandhian principle of nonviolence. Among the civil rights movement's ablest strategists, he served as a key resource for such major African-American leaders as Dr. King, James Farmer, Dorothy Height, Roy Wilkins, and Whitney Young.

In tracing the roots of Rustin's passion for nonviolence, his biographer, Jervis Anderson, related in *Bayard Rustin: Troubles I've Seen*:

[He] would remember growing up in a close-knit family, over which his grandmother Julia was the chief moral and religious influence—imparting values she had learned as a young Quaker. "We were told," Bayard said, "that we should never discuss an issue when we were wrought up, but only when we were calm. We were taught that it was too tiresome to hate, and that we should never go to sleep without first reconciling differences that had occurred during the day. We should never raise the question as to who had caused a dispute, for nothing constructive was to be gained by arguing over who started what."

Julia Rustin also emphasized the "simple" idea that no one was unimportant, "that it was our duty to treat each person as a complete human being."

Elizabeth Cady Stanton

••••••

On Social Reform

With her friend Lucretia Mott, abolitionist Elizabeth Cady Stanton organized the Women's Rights Convention at Seneca Falls, New York, in 1848. The mother of seven, Stanton struggled throughout her life to overturn what she saw as the most basic obstacle to women's equality: the prohibition of their right to vote. In editing an alternative version of Scripture that she called the *Women's Bible,* Stanton sought to offer a profeminist viewpoint. In the introduction, she wrote:

Let us remember that all reforms are interdependent, and that whatever is done to establish one principle on a solid basis, strengthens all. Reformers who are always compromising, have not yet grasped the idea that truth is the only safe ground to stand upon. The object of an individual life is not to carry one fragmentary measure in human progress, but to utter the highest truth clearly seen in all directions, and thus to round out and perfect a well-balanced character.

Julia Coleman and her pupil Jimmy Carter

On Encouraging Learning

Long after his tenure as thirty-ninth president of the United States, Jimmy Carter remains an active figure on the world scene. As a writer, public speaker, and volunteer international mediator, he continues to make his mark. Growing up in Depression-era rural Georgia, he was the son of a peanut farmer–businessman and a registered nurse.

Though Carter regarded both parents as contributing to his outlook and personal drive, in his 1975 campaign autobiography, entitled *Why Not the Best?,* the soon-to-be president highlighted, too, the inspirational guidance of a school superintendent, Miss Julia Coleman:

> Miss Julia was a spinster, who died recently, and she encouraged all of her students to seek cultural knowledge beyond the requirements of a normal rural school classroom. We were highly competitive in debating, an essay contest called "Ready Writing," music appreciation, one-act play productions, spelling bees, and other cultural activities.

Every student in the classroom was required to debate, to memorize and recite long poems and chapters from the Bible, and to participate in spelling contests. Each of us had to learn the rudiments of music and play some musical instrument—if it were only a ukulele, harmonica, or even a small piccolo.

Miss Julia remains alive in my memory. She was short and somewhat crippled, yet she was quite graceful as she moved along. Her face was expressive, particularly when she was reading one of the poems she loved, or presenting to a class the paintings of Millet, Gainesborough, Whistler, or Sir Joshua Reynolds.

When I was about twelve years old, she called me in and stated that she was ready for me to read *War and Peace*. I was happy with the title because I thought that finally Miss Julia had chosen for me a book about cowboys and Indians. I was appalled when I checked the book out of the library, because it was about 1,400 pages long, written by the Russian novelist Tolstoy, and of course, not about cowboys at all. [But] it turned out to be one of my favorite books.

Grandmother Page and her grandson
Dan Rather

●━━━━━━●

On the Importance of Reading

Born in rural Wharton, Texas, Dan Rather is one of America's leading television newscasters. His 1961 coverage of Hurricane Carla for Houston's CBS affiliate first impressed network higher-ups, who gave him a national slot. There Rather's reports on the JFK assassination, the Vietnam War, and Watergate steadily won him widespread acclaim, which increased after his on-air confrontations with an embattled, defensive President Nixon.

Rather has covered every Democratic and Republican convention since 1964 and has authored several books, including *The Camera Never Blinks*. In his memoir, *I Remember,* the popular broadcaster recalled:

> I am told that I was the first of the Pages or Rathers to make it through college, and I've given some thought to how I got there. . . .

Our matriarch, Grandmother Page, was of wagon breed, a big woman of unsurpassed energy. She was up at three-thirty or four o'clock in the morning, to bake and churn and get ready for the fields. At night, along with the cooking and sewing, there was energy left for her reading.

I doubt that Grandma Page went beyond the sixth grade in school, and hers was not a home filled with books. Sitting by her coal lamp, she read aloud to Mother from her precious copy of the Sears Roebuck catalog about garden seed and other items of home interest. . . .

By the time I came along, not much had changed except the edition of the catalog. Grandmother Page read me page after page from it. I don't remember that she ever ordered anything. The Sears catalog was her dream book. Its content wasn't about garden seed. It was about her dreams. . . .

I also believe she thought that the act of reading was important for deepening a child's interests. Grandma all but revered reading.

"Come, Danny, I'll read to you," she would say. That was enough to make me come running. It meant story time and story time most often was Bible time. The Bible was quite literally an open book for all the Rathers. You would rarely see a closed Bible in any of our homes. An open Bible meant that the good book was alive and well and had been lately in use. This was no pretense.

Grandma Page was well aware of my favorite Bible stories and catered to my taste for the great deeds it recorded, especially those of Joshua's at the Battle of Jericho. Meaning no disrespect for Grandma's religious beliefs, I should clarify that her bible offerings were meant less to serve the cause of piety than our need for entertainment. Joshua was my Sylvester Stallone, I guess . . . in [rural] Bloomington, Texas.

Johnnie Rowan and her son Carl

●●●●●●

On Support and Praise

Carl Rowan is one of America's most prominent African-American journalists today. In a career spanning over forty years, he has been an award-winning newspaper columnist, a panelist on television's *Inside Washington,* and a host of his own nationally syndicated radio program, *The Rowan Report*.

Raised in abject poverty in McMinnville, Tennessee, Rowan was among the first African-American officers in the U.S. Navy during World War II: Soon after, he gained national attention as a *Minneapolis Star* reporter covering the brutal reality of segregation in the Deep South. Later, in the 1960s, Rowan served as U.S. ambassador to Finland and as director of the U.S. Information Agency. He was the first African American to sit in cabinet meetings and on the U.S. National Security Council.

In Rowan's memoir, *Breaking Barriers,* the widely read syndicated columnist recalled his early years:

> Families buying precious food by the penny, the nickel, the dime, do not buy best-selling books or costly magazines. The only books my parents struggled to pay for were schoolbooks. I bless the memory of my mother sitting in a drafty and cold, or hot and humid, "livingroom," night after night, squinting by a flickering kerosene lamp, commanding me to "read this," "spell that," or "tell me what four times three is."
>
> She displayed an innate understanding that parental support and praise are wonderful stimulators of the self-respect, the yearning for knowledge, the willingness to work, of children at all levels of ability. I loved it beyond explanation or understanding when she would call off the words in my spelling book and, after I had spelled each correctly, would say to me, "There can't be anybody in that school smarter than you."

Leah Spielberg and her son Steven

•••••••

On Encouraging Self-Expression

Steven Spielberg is undoubtedly the most popular filmmaker in the world today. Since directing the blockbuster *Jaws* at the age of twenty-eight, he has directed a series of hugely profitable and artistically acclaimed movies, including *Close Encounters of the Third Kind, E.T., Raiders of the Lost Ark, The Color Purple, Jurassic Park,* and *Schindler's List.*

Spielberg grew up in a middle-class Jewish family in Cincinnati, Ohio, during the 1950s. Partly encouraged by his doting mother, Leah, the highly imaginative young Steven began to make amateur films and received constant support for this self-expression. In *Steven Spielberg,* Joseph McBride related:

> Because of Steven's extreme precocity, the Spielberg family rabbi, Fishel Goldfelder, felt impelled to offer Leah advice on how to deal with her unusual son. One day, the rabbi saw Steven

throwing a tantrum because he wanted a toy, perhaps a fire truck. He raised a big fuss. Rabbi Goldfelder said to Leah, "Buy it for him, you're going to buy it for him anyway."

Leah took the rabbi's advice.... "Nobody ever said no to Steven," she recalled decades later. "He always gets what he wants, anyway, so the name of the game [was] to save your strength and say yes early." Asked how she influenced her son's development, Leah replied: "I gave him freedom.

"And everything Steven wanted to do, he did. We lived very spur of the moment; there was no structure. He has an amazing talent—this cannot be denied—but he also had the freedom to express it."

Maria Montessori

●━━━━●

On the Learning Process

One of the most influential educators of the modern era, Maria Montessori was born in 1870 in Italy. She became the first woman in her country's history to receive a medical degree when she graduated from the University of Rome. In the late 1890s Montessori began working extensively with preschool children both with and, later, without disabilities. She founded her first school in 1907, pioneering a host of innovations emphasizing youngsters' natural ability to learn. She especially valued individualized and hands-on activities, rather than group lockstep and rote memorization. Today hundreds of early-childhood programs throughout the world are based upon Montessori educational methods.

In her book *The Absorbent Mind* (1949) Montessori looked back on her fifty-year career and declared:

Ours was a house for children, rather than a real school. We had prepared a place for children where a diffused culture could be assimilated, without any need for direct instruction. Yet, these children learned to read and write before they were five, and no one had given them any lessons. At that time, it seemed miraculous that children of four-and-a-half should be able to write, and that they should have learned without the feeling of having been taught.

We puzzled over it for a long time. Only after repeated experiments did we conclude with certainty that all children are endowed with this capacity to "absorb" culture. If this be true—we then argued— if culture can be acquired without effort, let us provide the children with other elements of culture. And then we saw them "absorb" far more than reading and writing: botany, zoology, mathematics, geography,

and all with the same ease, spontaneously and without getting tired.

And so we discovered that education is not something which the teacher does, but that it is a natural process which develops spontaneously in the human being. It is not acquired by listening to words, but in virtue of experiences in which the child acts on his environment. The teacher's task is not to talk, but to prepare and arrange a series of motives for cultural activity in a special environment made for the child.

Ruby Dandridge and her daughter Dorothy

━━━━━━

On Encouraging Talent

Dorothy Dandridge—like Marilyn Monroe and Elizabeth Taylor—was a Hollywood dream goddess of the 1950s. With unforgettable beauty and screen magnetism, she was also the nation's first full-fledged African-American movie star. She won an Academy Award nomination for best actress in Otto Preminger's *Carmen Jones;* Dandridge also starred in such films as *Porgy and Bess* and *Island in the Sun*. More than anyone else, she broke Hollywood's prevailing stereotype of the comic "mammy" role for African-American women.

Talented from the start, Dandridge began her career as a little girl in Cleveland in an act that her mother, Ruby, an actress and comedian, created for her. This act was the stepping-stone to stage, and then film roles by her teens. In *Dorothy Dandridge,* Donald Bogle recounted:

As a preschool child, Dorothy watched closely as her mother memorized and rehearsed poetry, usually by one of Ruby's favorites, African American writer Paul Lawrence Dunbar. Dorothy sat engrossed in Ruby's every move, mood, gesture, vocal inflection, and change of expression.

One evening when an exhausted Ruby returned home from work, she matter-of-factly told her daughter that she was too tired to perform at a scheduled engagement. "I'll do it for you, Mama," said Dorothy. . . .

[Ruby's] four-year-old daughter stood in the kitchen and recited Dunbar's lines word for word, and in the very manner she had watched her mother do it. . . .

Ruby Dandridge, with her infallible instincts, immediately decided to let Dorothy go in her place. At the church that evening, she observed that Dorothy was an adorable little crowd-pleaser whose letter-perfect performance delighted the adults in the audience. . . .

"You ain't going to work in Mister Charley's kitchen like me," was what Dorothy remembered Ruby telling her time and again. "I don't want you to go into service. You're not going to be a scullery maid. We're gonna fix it so you be something else than that." Show business could be a way out—and up. And thanks to Dorothy's mother, it certainly became so.

Donna Ficker and her daughter
Suzanne Farrell

●━━●━━●━━●

On Developing Ability

As a child Roberta Sue Ficker of Cincinnati, Ohio, never dreamed she would become Suzanne Farrell, the youngest ballerina in the history of the New York City Ballet. With a tomboy demeanor, she much enjoyed tree climbing, dodgeball, and playing "dress-up"—and envisioned a career as a clown. But after several years of ballet lessons "Suzanne" was discovered at age fourteen by New York City choreographer George Balanchine, and in 1961 began dancing featured roles with his School of American Ballet. Until she retired from the stage in 1989, the tall, graceful dancer gained international acclaim in such productions as *Don Quixote, Swan Lake, Romeo and Juliet, Bolero,* and the highly praised *Nijinsky, Clown of God*.

In her autobiography, *Holding On to the Air,* Farrell, who is still active worldwide as a ballet teacher, reminisced about the source of her success:

Mother came from a self-supporting family, where work was work and play was work. If any of us weren't good at what we were being taught (as I wasn't at painting), those lessons ended. Her overwhelming belief in us didn't blind her. She was pursuing rather impractical interests in a practical manner, and that's probably one very good reason why I was able to become what I became. . . .

Mother was not a typical stage mother. She made lessons available to us, but she never watched class, never hung around commenting on our progress. She had been lonely as a child, and perhaps she knew that if you have the arts in your life, you will never be lonely. I have often been alone, but I have never felt lonely when I was dancing, even dancing by myself.

Abigail Alcott and her daughter Louisa May

●●●●●●

On Guiding Interests

Louisa May Alcott is best known for her enduring novel *Little Women*. Published soon after the end of the U.S. Civil War, it tells the vivid story of four sisters growing up in a New England town during the mid-1800s. Its depiction of family life from a woman's perspective made it an immediate success: The novel gave Alcott lifetime financial security and a platform for her later activism on social issues ranging from temperance to women's voting rights.

Raised in Boston and Concord, Massachusetts, by educated and free-thinking parents, Louisa showed writing talent at an early age. In 1839 her mother, Abigail, penned this loving letter:

Dear Daughter,

Your tenth birthday has arrived. May it be a happy one, and on each returning birthday may you feel new strength and resolution to be gentle with sisters, obedient to parents, loving to everyone, and happy in yourself.

I give you the pencil-case I promised, for I have observed that you are fond of writing, and wish to encourage the habit.

Go on trying, dear, and each day it will be easier to be and do good. You must help yourself, for the cause of your little troubles is in yourself; and patience and courage only will make you what Mother prays to see you—her good and happy girl.

Undoubtedly seeing her daughter's interest in writing continue to grow, Louisa's mother offered these sentiments on Louisa's eleventh birthday:

Your handwriting improves very fast. Take pains and do not be in a hurry. I like to have you make observations about our conversation and your own thoughts. It helps you to express them and to understand your little self. Remember, dear girl, that a diary should be an epitome of your life. May it be a record of pure thought and good actions, then you will indeed be the precious child of your loving mother.

Kamala Nehru and her daughter
Indira Gandhi

●━━━━━●

On Fighting for Equality

Indira Gandhi served as India's first female prime minister for eleven
years, from 1966 to 1977; she held the office again from 1980 to 1984.
Earlier, as minister of information and broadcasting in Lal Bahadur
Shastri's government, she helped to dismantle the prevailing censorship and approved a television education project in family planning.

Indira was born to Jawaharal Nehru, India's first prime minister
and an associate of Mahatma Gandhi. Arrested by the British on
charges of subversion, Indira spent thirteen months in prison but
resumed her ceaseless activism on her release. Before reaching the age
of forty she was elected to the executive body of the Congress Party
and steadily rose through its ranks. As biographer Inder Malhotra
states in *Indira Gandhi: A Personal and Political Biography,* her mother
was an inspirational figure:

By temperament and upbringing, Kamala was better suited than the luxury-loving Nehrus to the austerity that Gandhi preached. Not only did she lend full emotional support to her husband when frequently arrested and imprisoned, Kamala became joyfully committed to actively helping them, and indeed, she took upon herself the task of expanding the nationalist struggle unleashed by Mahatma Gandhi.

As a bright child, Indira certainly saw this development. Decades later, she proudly told a women's seminar, "Many people know the part which was played by my grandfather and my father. But, in my opinion, a more important part was played by my mother. When my father wanted to join Gandhi and to change the whole way of life . . . the whole family was against it. It was only my mother's courageous and persistent support and encouragement that enabled him to take this step which made such a difference not only to our family, but the history of modern India."

Jacqueline Kennedy Onassis

◆◆◆◆◆◆

On Fostering Creativity

When Jacqueline Kennedy Onassis died shortly before her sixty-fifth birthday, she left behind an unforgettable legacy. Certainly Jackie was admired for her accomplishments as an influential book editor and tireless spokesperson for the arts in the United States. However, she is probably best remembered by her family—and the entire stunned nation—for her quiet dignity in the aftermath of President John F. Kennedy's assassination in 1963. Raising her two children, Caroline and John, to maturity was a challenging venture for Jackie. She once said, "The things you do with your children, you never forget."

When asked about her child-rearing philosophy Jackie stated in *Jacqueline Kennedy Onassis: A Portrait in Her Own Words,* by Bill Adler, the importance of nurturing imagination and creativity:

> Perhaps some painting—just some splattering of watercolors or crayon lines the way a child loves to do it—is the first step.

Whenever I paint now, I put up a child's paint box for Caroline beside me. She really prefers to dip the brushes in water, smear the paints, and make a mess, but it is a treat for her to paint with her mother.

Perhaps this will develop a latent talent; perhaps it will merely do what it did for me, produce occasional paintings which only one's family could admire, and be a source of pleasure and relaxation.

When I was a child, my mother helped us enormously with our creative instincts. . . .

When I was ten years old, I memorized "The Vision of Sir Launfal" by James Russell Lowell for my mother's birthday. It was eleven pages long in my poetry book and I was enormously proud of myself at the time. I can still remember whole passages of it today.

I mention these examples to show that a mind, trained young to retain, continues to do so.

Julia Wolfe and her son Thomas

●●●●●●●

On Helping with Schoolwork

Though he lived only thirty-eight years Thomas Wolfe achieved fame
for his autobiographical novels, including *Look Homeward, Angel; Of
Time and the River;* and the posthumously published *You Can't Go
Home Again.* With startling yet tender poetic imagery, Wolfe's writing
was often disorganized but carried great emotional impact.

Wolfe grew up in small-town Asheville, North Carolina, before the
first World War. It was not a milieu that favored literary precocity, but
his mother, Julia, saw his talent early on and zealously encouraged it.
Not long after Thomas's death she reminisced in *Thomas Wolfe's
Letters to his Mother, Julia Elizabeth Wolfe,* edited by John Terry, about
their lifelong close relationship:

> While we were on a holiday at St. Petersburg, I took [Tom]
> over to the school and the teacher was very anxious for him to
> enter. But they found that his books were all different [from

theirs] and [theirs would] cost considerable. Tom said to me, "We don't know what might happen. We might not stay here very long and that's just extra expense, buying all those books I won't have any use for when I get back home, for they're different from ours. I have my own books with me. Suppose I study and *you* be my teacher?"

I asked him, "Will you do that?"

He said, "Yes."

Well, we had our lessons every morning. He often laughed. He said, "Mama, don't you know you're giving long lessons?"

I said, "Why, you can study those lessons!" He [agreed], "They're not too long."

He did study them. There weren't any too long for him. He said they were much longer than the teacher in Asheville gave him. And we got back home and he entered in the same class. Then I noticed something one day and said, "Tom, don't you bring any books home?"

He [proudly] said, "Don't have to. It'll be a month before they catch up to where we studied when we were in St. Petersburg."

Caroline Darwin and her younger brother Charles

———————

On Recognizing Improvement

Charles Darwin was an English naturalist who became famous for his theories on evolution. Published in 1859, his *On the Origin of Species by Means of Natural Selection* is among the world's most influential scientific works. Charles's mother died when he was only eight years old and, because his father never remarried, his older sister Caroline became a surrogate mother. She took interest and pleasure in her gifted brother's developing scientific career, and the two corresponded regularly after he began traveling as a naturalist-explorer.

Darwin, twenty-four, was aboard the English expedition ship H.M.S. *Beagle* when Caroline penned him this useful and encouraging literary advice:

> I have been reading with the greatest interest your journal and found it very entertaining and interesting. Your writing at the

time gives such reality to your descriptions and brings every little incident before one with a force that no after-account could do. I am very doubtful whether it is not pert in me to criticize, using merely my own judgment, for no one else in the family has yet read this last part—but I will say just what I think—I mean as to your style.

I thought in the first part (of your last journal) that you had, probably from reading so much of Humboldt, got his phraseology and occasionally made use of the kind of flowery French expressions which he uses, instead of your own simple, straightforward and far more agreeable style. I have no doubt you have without perceiving it got to embody your ideas in his poetical language, and from his being a foreigner, it does not sound unnatural in him.

Remember, this criticism only applies to parts of your journal, the greatest part I liked exceedingly and could find no fault, and all of it I had the greatest pleasure in reading.

Filia Holtzman and her daughter Elizabeth

■■■■■■■

On Social Involvement

Born in Brooklyn, New York, and graduating from Harvard Law School, Elizabeth Holtzman has devoted most of her adult life to public service. At thirty-one she toppled Emmanuel Celler, a fifty-year veteran of the U.S. House of Representatives, and subsequently served four terms in Congress. Her causes included prohibiting sex discrimination in federal programs and revising immigration policies. Following an unsuccessful bid for a U.S. Senate seat against Republican contender Alfonse D'Amato in 1980, Holtzman served eight years as Brooklyn's district attorney, and later as comptroller of New York City.

In her autobiography, *Who Said It Would Be Easy?,* Holtzman warmly recalled:

> My mother and her family came from Bielaya Tserkov in the Ukraine when she was twelve. . . .

Because my mother was fluent in Russian, she was recruited during World War II to work in a classified job in the Office of Censorship. When she completed her Ph.D. in Russian, she began teaching evening classes at Brooklyn College, and later she taught at Hunter College, becoming the head of the department. Her decision to pursue a career was completely natural, never in question. Our house brimmed with academic hubbub. College students were constantly in and out of our living room for serious teas with meaningful discussions, and professor colleagues of my mother's often joined us for dinner. Everyone greeted my mother with tremendous respect.

Deeply concerned about social justice, my mother joined picket lines when she could to support workers fighting against labor inequities. She let us know that violence was to be rebuffed and told me how disturbing she found racism in America. And I can remember in grade school coming home from school and sitting with my mother as she watched the McCarthy hearings on television in dismay. From an early age, I fully understood that serious injustices were occurring.

Madeleine L'Engle

―――――

On Providing Clear Rules of Conduct

Madeleine L'Engle is the author of more than forty-five books for all ages, including the beloved children's fantasy *A Wrinkle in Time*. She has won numerous awards for both fiction and nonfiction, and lectures to civic, educational, and religious groups on her literary themes. An only child who grew up in 1920s New York City, L'Engle was exposed a great deal to reading and culture. After touring briefly as a professional actress, she devoted herself full time to writing and raising a large family in rural Connecticut.

In a freewheeling memoir titled *A Circle of Quiet,* L'Engle shared many insights about child rearing, personal development, and family life.

L'Engle and her husband Hugh, who were already parents of young children, took in the child of friends who had died suddenly. The seven-year-old girl was confused and angry over the death of her parents and, as L'Engle put it, the girl wanted to test the cosmos to prove that there was a structure to life. After months of kindness, patience, and steady discipline, the girl continued to act out against her new foster family. In a moment of insight, L'Engle and her husband stopped making the girl do her chores; the girl didn't have to make her bed or set the table. She could do what she wanted. Frightened that the security of their loving discipline was gone, it wasn't long before the child was sneaking into the dining room to set the table. L'Engle comments on parenting in this way:

> Sometimes Hugh and I feel that if we have done anything right with our children it has been accident and a miracle; often we realize in retrospect, that the things we thought were best weren't really very good at all. Perhaps our children have taught themselves more on our mistakes than on our good will. But we still have the courage to make decisions, to say yes, here; no, there.

Adelle Maxwell and her grandson Bill Gates

●━●━●━●━●━●

On Thinking Smart

As cofounder and chief executive of Microsoft, Bill Gates has become one of the world's richest men. Growing up in an affluent Seattle family in the 1960s, he showed intellectual brilliance at an early age, and his private school teachers struggled to keep him challenged and meaningfully occupied. Gates's father was a successful corporate lawyer putting in long hours at work, and his mother was equally active in civic and other volunteer activities. The family was closely knit, but as a recent biography by Stephen Masnes and Paul Andrews titled, simply, *Gates* reveals, his maternal grandmother played a vital role in his upbringing:

> Adelle Maxwell, known as "Gam," was there to greet him and his sister when they came home and their mother was out volunteering. That was often. . . . So Gam assumed the after-school duties, making sure to disappear just before Bill Jr. came home

so that she wouldn't be seen as an intrusive mother-in-law. Neighborhood children thought of Gam as a surrogate mom, always ready with cookies and conversation when their mothers needed time off to shop or run errands.

There was a reason Adelle Maxwell dubbed her grandson "Trey": She loved games, particularly cards, and taught young Bill double solitaire, fish, gin, bridge, and a variety of other favorites. For Gam, who had been a star forward on the women's basketball team at Enumclaw High School, as well as class valedictorian, games were not frivolous diversions but tests of skill and intelligence. "Very early on we played bridge," Mary Gates remembered, "and she was always saying to him, 'Think smart, think smart.'"

Games of all sorts were a constant in the competitive Gates household—everything from board games to jigsaw puzzle competitions. After dinner, the family would often play cards to see who would do the dishes. Perhaps the ultimate moment in Gatesian gaming legend came when Mary and Bill Jr. learned of her unexpected pregnancy. The parents broke the news to Trey and Kristi in Gam's living room via the medium of Hangman. Before the noose won out, the kids guessed the message: "A little visitor is coming soon." Bill's sister Libby was born in June 1964.

Adelle's intellectual quickness was a major influence on Trey. Gam often read books to the kids, and Bill became an avid reader with broad interests: Math and science books vied for his attention with such classic juvenile fiction as *Charlotte's Web, Dr. Dolittle,* and the Freddie the Pig, Tom Swift, and Tarzan series. A public library near his home had summer reading contests; as Gates recalled, he was always the first among the boys, and occasionally even first among the girls.

After Gam's death in 1987, Mary Gates recalled, the family gathered in the living room of their son's new residential complex. There he spoke movingly of his grandmother. "I haven't forgotten that he described her as the most principled person he had ever known. And I think that her standards and values were great five-point star inspirations for him."

The Queen of Sheba

On Challenging the Mind

In the Hebrew Bible there is only brief mention of the Queen of Sheba, who became one of King Solomon's most acclaimed wives. However, in the Jewish legendary tradition known as the Midrash, the Queen of Sheba is presented far more fully. Not only was her beauty unequalled but, according to this fascinating tradition, she also challenged Solomon with twenty-two riddles in order to test his wisdom and, ultimately, his worthiness as a mate.

The queen's baffling questions, extracted from *Legends of the Bible* by Louis Ginzburg, all answered correctly by the ardent Hebrew king, included the following:

"Seven there are that issue and nine that enter; two yield the draught and one drinks." His reply: "Seven are the days of a woman's menstrual period and nine the months of pregnancy; two are the breasts that yield the draught, and one the child that drinks it."

"A woman said to her son, your father is my father, and your grandfather my husband; you are my son, and I am your sister." His reply: "Assuredly, it was the daughter of Lot who spoke thus to her son."

"Who is he who neither was born nor has died?" His reply: "It is the Lord of the world, blessed be He."

"There is something which when living moves, yet when its head is cut off, it moves." His reply: "It is the ship on the sea."

"Who were the three that ate and drank on the earth, and yet were not born of male and female?" His reply: "The three angels who visited Abraham."

"What was that which was not born, yet life was given to it?" His reply: "The golden calf."

"What is that which is produced from the ground, yet humans produce it, while its food is the fruit on the ground?" His reply: "A wick."

"A house full of dead; no dead one came among them, nor did a living come forth from them." His reply: "It is the story of Samson and the Philistines."

"What is this? It walks ahead of all; it cries out loud and bitterly; its head is like the reed; it is the glory of the noble, the disgrace of the poor; the glory of the dead, the disgrace of the living; the delight of birds; the distress of fishes." Solomon's apt reply: "Flax."

Golda Meir and her son Menachem

●●●●●●●

On the Value of Democracy

Golda Meir served as prime minister of Israel from 1969 to 1974 and held several other key cabinet posts during her long career. Born in Ukraine, she emigrated as a child with her family to Milwaukee, Wisconsin, in 1906, and later taught school there. She relocated to the Holy Land in the early 1920s and became steadily more active in political affairs while raising two children in a difficult marriage.

In his memoir, *My Mother, Golda Meir,* her son, Menachem, recalled:

> With all this [happening in Tel Aviv], there was also the world of our home, a home, which despite everything, was warm and well run. . . .
>
> When Mother was with us, she was really there; attentive, kind, considerate, witty and a healer of wounds. I never felt that I was second to her other interests, or that I was being neglected for the sake of her ego or personal advancement. Whenever she

left the house, she explained—according to our age and ability to understand—exactly where she was going, and why.

I remember an evening when I must have been six and Mother had left for a Labor Party meeting after telling us she'd be home early. Sarah and I just couldn't fall asleep. We talked and giggled, went through our repertoire of songs, and then when Mother still hadn't gotten back, we dressed and marched off to fetch her from party headquarters.

She was standing up in front, counting raised hands, so we too raised our hands, hoping to be noticed and wanting to participate. Mother smiled and beckoned, and when the meeting ended, she introduced us—as she would increasingly in later years—to all her colleagues. On the way home, she put into simple words what the meeting had been about and what those raised hands meant. Actually, I think, it was our first lesson in the political life of a democracy.

Maybelle Mitchell and her daughter Margaret

●━━●━●━●━●

On the Value of Education

Gone with the Wind, which won the Pulitzer Prize in 1937 and was made two years later into a remarkably popular movie, reflected author Margaret Mitchell's origins and milieu. Born in 1900 to a fifth-generation Georgian, she worked as a reporter for the *Atlanta Journal* before resigning in 1926 to begin writing what would become her only full-length book. It took nine years for her to find a publisher and see the novel's release to American readers, but it sold a million copies within its first six months.

Vividly set in Civil War and Reconstruction Georgia, *Gone with the Wind* became an American entertainment phenomenon, offering such memorable characters as beautiful Scarlett O'Hara and dastardly Rhett Butler. Though Mitchell maintained a voluminous correspondence, she never published another novel and tragically died in a car accident at the age of forty-nine.

As her biographer Anne Edwards vividly recounted in *Road to Tara: The Life of Margaret Mitchell,* the bestselling author was strongly influenced by her mother:

Returning from her first day at North Boulevard School, Margaret told her mother that she had arithmetic and did not want to go back. Maybelle ordered Margaret into the Mitchells' stylish horse-drawn carriage, took the reins herself, and drove out toward Clayton County and the Fitzgerald farm at such a clip that Margaret gripped the seat in fear. . . .

"Fine and wealthy people once lived in those houses," she told the child, slowing the horses and pointing at the shabby former plantation houses that they passed. "Now they are old ruins and some of them have been that way since Sherman marched through. Some fell to pieces when the families in them fell to pieces. See that one there?" she said as she passed a derelict farmstead. "The people who lived in that house were ruined with it."

She wheeled the trembling child around to look toward the opposite side of the road and motioned to an old but well-tended dwelling. "Now, those folks stood as staunchly as their house did. You remember that, child—that the world those people lived in was a secure world, just like yours is now. Your world will do that to you one day, too, and God help you, child, if you don't have some weapon to meet that new world. Education!"

Maybelle bellowed in a voice that cut the silence of the country twilight. "People—and especially women—might as well consider they are lost without an education, both classical and political. For all you're going to be left with after your world up-ends will be what you do with your hands and what you have in your head. You will go back to school tomorrow," she ended [firmly,] "and you will conquer arithmetic."

And with that, she let go of her daughter, grasped the reins, and, turning around, cracked the buggy whip and started swiftly and silently on the long ride home.

Anne James and her son Henry

On the Value of Travel

Over a fifty-year career Henry James produced twenty novels, including *The Americans, The Europeans, Washington Square,* and *Portrait of a Lady*. He grew up in a wealthy, cosmopolitan family in New York City. His parents, Anne and William, believed in providing James and his four siblings with a self-directed education. In a letter dated July 1869, Anne sent twenty-six-year-old James the following advice.

My dear beloved child, your letter last evening opens the deepest fountains in my soul, and my bosom seems as if it must burst with its burden of love and tenderness. If you were only here, and we could talk over this subject of expense, I could, I know, exorcise all those demons of anxiety and conscientiousness that possess you, and leave you free as air to enjoy to the full all that surrounds you, and drink in health of body and mind in following out your own safe and innocent attractions.

Living

Mary Beard and her son James

·······

On Appreciating Cuisine

James Beard was one of America's most revered master chefs and teachers of modern cooking. Raised in Oregon, he spent several years abroad studying voice and theater, but finally abandoned his faltering acting career in 1935 to start a catering business. Success came quickly, and he published the first of many cookbooks five years later.

After World War II ended Beard settled in New York City, appeared on television's first cooking show on NBC in 1946, and eventually became a household name for advocating a cuisine based on fresh, wholesome, American ingredients. Until his death in 1985 he directed the James Beard Cooking School and lectured tirelessly to women's clubs, cooking schools, and civic groups.

In *Epicurean Delight,* biographer Evan Jones recounted how influential James's mother had been in his life:

James busied himself more and more in the kitchen—burning but then mastering bread by age eight—and continued his cultural education under Mary. [Before long], James was old enough to accompany Mary on some of her trips away from Portland. . . . Now at least once a year, [they] would go by train or ship to San Francisco to gorge themselves on the arts, food, and the fascinating people Mary knew there: actors, decorators, singers, and strong women like herself in the hospitality business. . . .

But above all, there was food in sophisticated company at Solari's, sumptuous buffet lunches at Marquand's, tea under the glass-covered central court of the Palace Hotel, crab, sand dabs, and abalone at Jack's, and dinner among the city's glamour brigade at Tair's.

". . . I think about Mother's small woodstove at [our summer cottage] at Gearhart, Oregon," Beard wrote late in life, "and the dishes that issued from that tiny kitchen. I still wonder at her technique. . . . Her hand was an infallible gauge."

In his seventies, Beard fondly recalled the summer picnics she masterfully accomplished. . . . "Those busy days on the Oregon coast left their mark on me, and no place on earth, with the exception of Paris, has done as much to influence my professional life."

Virginia Runner and her grandson
Clint Eastwood

●━●━●━●

On Love for Nature

Tall, soft-spoken, and with a leathery countenance, Clint Eastwood has become one of Hollywood's most venerated figures. He grew up in depression-era California, where his parents were itinerant workers. After high school he worked as a lumberjack in Oregon, played honky-tonk piano, and was a swimming instructor in the United States Army. Eastwood studied at Los Angeles City College on the GI Bill and, after working in many B movies, gained national recognition for his role as trail boss Rowdy Yates in the successful television series *Rawhide*.

Following his starring roles in Spanish director Sergio Leone's "spaghetti westerns," including *A Fistful of Dollars,* Eastwood gained wide popularity for his Dirty Harry character portrayal. In 1992 Eastwood won two Oscars and several other major awards for acting in and directing the western *Unforgiven*.

In *Clint Eastwood: A Biography,* Richard Schickel recounts how Eastwood's maternal grandmother, Virginia Runner, was a key influence during his formative, impoverished years:

> The Eastwoods [often stayed in] a semirural community where Mrs. Runner, then working as a bookkeeper for a food-processing company, could live in solitary confinement. A largehearted, sweetly eccentric woman, warm in her affections, [she] set . . . for Clint a memorable, often-cited example of the independent life. Clint and his sister lived with her once for an entire school year during a particularly unsettled period, Clint happily sleeping in a tent he had pitched in the backyard. Afterward, he visited her as often as he could.
>
> Clint attributes his lifelong affection for animals to his grandmother, for there was always a shifting population of pets in and around her house. It may be that her move, a little later in Clint's childhood, to seven acres of land, mostly given over to olive trees, near Sunol, was motivated by her desire to support a more extensive menagerie [of farm animals and pets]. . . .
>
> He also remembers that on his visits to his grandmother, he was able to range the nearby hills on long solitary walks, on which he acted all kinds of imaginary adventures.

Finally, though, the most important thing he took away from his visits with his grandmother was her uncomplicated faith that there was something special about him. . . .

Alone among Clint's extended family, she predicted a bright future within a creative field for this seemingly ordinary boy. Virginia firmly noted that her grandson had "long hands," which to her, bespoke a natural gift for the arts. This proved to be a prescient observation, because Clint's use of his hands—graceful, precise, and sometimes rather startling in the context of some of his roles—is one of the hallmarks of his acting style. Virginia did not live to see him become a movie star, but she did watch him become a television star on *Rawhide*. "And she never let anyone forget it."

Edith Bawden and her granddaughter Nina

●━━━━●

On Storytelling

Nina Bawden, one of England's most popular and prolific novelists, was born in 1925 London. She studied at Oxford University and worked in town and country planning. She has written several novels for adults including *Who Calls the Tune, Under the Skin,* and *Circles of Deceit,* which was made into a television movie in 1980. Bawden has also published several children's adventure stories, such as *The Witch's Daughter* and her most successful work, *Carrie's War*.

In her recent memoir, *In My Own Time,* the writer traced the origin of her literary ability:

> I was lucky to have known my grandmother, and lucky that she had a good memory and a talent for stories. And a robust common sense. . . .
>
> My grandmother was older than any other grown-up around me, which set her apart from them, and she didn't behave as they

did. Specifically, she never assumed any authority over me, or at any rate, none that I was conscious of. I thought of her as another child like me, albeit rather old. She was ready to play draughts [checkers], go to the cinema, more or less whenever I wanted. And she was always ready to tell stories—anxious to, indeed, which is probably the key to the comfortable relationship between us. What I wanted from her, she wanted to give me, and there was never any feeling on my part that she was tailoring her stories to fit my younger understanding: censoring them in any way.

Abigail Adams and her son
John Quincy Adams

❖❖❖❖❖❖

On Aiming High

Abigail Adams has a unique status in American history. An influential patriot during the Revolutionary War, she was also married to one president (John Adams) and mother to a second (John Quincy Adams). Born in Weymouth, Massachusetts, to a family of Congregational ministers, Abigail lacked formal education (as did other women of her time). But her curiosity sparked her keen intelligence, and she read widely.

Long separations kept Abigail from her beloved husband, John, while he served as delegate to the Continental Congress, envoy abroad, and elected officer under the newly crafted Constitution. The two were married for more than fifty years and raised five children. Respected for speaking forthrightly on many contemporary issues, Abigail offered this insightful advice to twelve-year-old John Quincy in January 1780:

These are times in which a genius would wish to live. It is not in the still calm of life, or the repose of a pacific station, that great characters are formed. Would Cicero have shone so distinguished an orator, if he had not been roused, kindled, and enflamed by the tyranny of Catiline, Millo, Verres, and Mark Anthony? The habits of a vigorous mind are formed in contending with difficulties. All history will convince you of this, and that wisdom and penetration are the fruits of experience, not the lessons of retirement and leisure.

Great necessities all out great virtues. When a mind is raised, and animated by scenes that engage the heart, then those qualities which would otherwise lay dormant, wake into life, and form the character of the hero and the statesman.

Miss Martin and her pupil Isaac Asimov

•••••••

On Recovering from Failure

Isaac Asimov, who authored several hundred books, is best known for his science fiction stories and novels. These included the futuristic *I, Robot*; *Fantastic Voyage*; and *Foundation* series. Trained as a chemist, he also served as a scientific consultant to the original *Star Trek* television series. Emigrating as a child with his family to Brooklyn from Russia in the winter of 1923, he showed a gifted but unruly mind. Asimov's parents, uneducated and hardworking, were often impatient, exasperated, and punitive with him.

In his multivolume autobiography—the first titled *In Memory Yet Green*—Asimov gratefully recalled the influence of his fifth-grade teacher, identified simply as Miss Martin:

> She was the best teacher I had. . . . She was unfailingly good-natured and never scolded shrewishly.
>
> Miss Martin liked me. For one thing she gave me the oppor-

tunity to recover from a particularly painful setback I had had in [a spelling bee]. When it was time for the term's spelling bee, Miss Martin asked the class if there was anyone interested in representing the class. When I did not raise my hand, Miss Martin asked why.

The class looked at me. I said, "I [lost] last term, Miss Martin. I don't think the class wants me."

Miss Martin said to the class, "Isaac has the best marks for spelling in this term, and I think he can win. How many in the class want him?"

Once she expressed her preference, of course, all the little sycophants raised a cry on my behalf, and I was forced to be the 5B1 representative in a bee that included all the classes in the fourth, fifth, and sixth grades.

I was nervous again, but this time, at least, I had the comforting knowledge that I could not do worse than the term before. As soon as I spelled the first word correctly, I was ahead of the game . . . and I won. I got a fountain pen as my prize, the first one I had ever owned. . . .

She was *such* a softhearted teacher. I saw her once or twice during the next year, but then I left PS 202 and I never saw or heard from her again. Still—thank you, Miss Martin, wherever you are.

Natalia Ginzburg

●●●●●●●

On Acknowledging Any Possibility

The child of socialist parents, Natalia Ginzburg was forced to live under Fascist rule in Abruzzi during World War II. She became Italy's most important postwar woman writer, compared in stature to Alberto Moravia and the late Italo Calvino. Her books include *Family Sayings, The Road to the City,* and *All Our Yesterdays*. Ginzburg also served as a member of the Italian Parliament and a translator of French literature. This selection on parenting is taken from her book *The Little Virtues:*

> As far as the education of children is concerned, I think they should be taught not the little virtues but the great ones. Not thrift but generosity and an indifference to money; not caution but courage and a contempt for danger; not shrewdness but frankness and a love of truth; not tact but love for one's neighbor and self-denial; not a desire for success but a desire to be and to know.

In these days, when a dialogue between parents and their children has become possible—possible though always difficult, always complicated by mutual prejudices, bashfulness, inhibitions—it is necessary that in this dialogue we show ourselves for what we are, imperfect, in the hope that our children will not resemble us but be stronger and better than us.

What we must remember above all in the education of our children is that their love of life should never weaken. This love can take different forms.... We should not demand anything, we should not ask or hope that he is a genius or an artist or a hero or a saint; and yet we must be ready for everything; our waiting and our patience must compass both the possibility of the highest and the most ordinary of fates.

Minnie Bourke and her daughter Margaret

On Choosing the Hard Way

Margaret Bourke-White ranks as one of America's greatest photographers. With positions at *Fortune* and *Life* magazines, she became a national figure in the 1930s and 1940s. Her award-winning photographs focused on such themes as rural poverty in America, life in Russia under Nazi attack, conditions in Mahatma Gandhi's India and apartheid South Africa during the post-World War II era.

Raised by doting but career-oriented parents in Bound Brook, New Jersey, Margaret was especially influenced by her mother, Minnie, who worked in publishing. In her autobiography, *Portrait of Myself,* the famous photographer recalled:

> The love of truth is requisite Number 1 for a photographer. And in this training, Mother [was a key figure]. When I was a

very small child, if I broke a soup plate, Mother would say, "Margaret, was it an accident or was it carelessness?" If I said it was carelessness, I was punished; an accident, I was forgiven. I am proud of Mother's vision in knowing how important [it was] to learn to be the judge of one's own behavior. She did well to see that a habit of truth throughout life is more important than the broken soup plates.

Some of her rules, I believe now in retrospect, were unnecessarily Spartan, but this judgment is made affectionately, for mixed in with the strict regulations there was so much that was good. . . .

If my sister or I took one of those school examinations where you are required to answer only ten questions out of twelve, Mother's comment on hearing of this would be, "I hope you chose the ten hardest ones." Reject the easy path! Do it the hard way!

Caro McWilliams and her daughter
Julia Child

●●●●●●●

On Becoming Your Own Person

Julia Child is among the best-known cooking experts in the world. Over the past thirty-five years she has authored such bestsellers as *Mastering the Art of French Cooking, The Way to Cook,* and *Cooking With Master Chefs.* She has hosted many shows on television, including the thirty-nine-part series *Baking at Julia's,* which ran in 1996. Raised in Pasadena, California, between the two World Wars, Child began her culinary training at the relatively late age of thirty-seven at Paris's famed Cordon Bleu. But, as a biographer Noël Fitch recounts in *Appetite for Life,* her high-spirited, warm, and outgoing personality was greatly influenced by her free-spirited mother:

> In her affluent community, Julia's mother was regarded as a finely-polished woman of decorum. But to her friends and later

her adult children, she was Caro—a spontaneous woman who loved petting dogs, playing tennis, and chatting with friends. She was no Victorian matriarch who occupied her time in domestic concerns. Caro never taught her daughters to sew or to manicure their nails. But she surrounded them with her approval, showing them how to love sports, laughter, and friends, and follow one's interests. . . .

Her famous daughter Julia recounted that "We loved her and we did lots of things with her. She was usually there when we came home from school; she was more like a friend than a mother. I remember as kiddies we would all lie on the couch and Mother would read to us. I remember she was reading us something like *Bob, Son of Battle,* and we three were sobbing. She was very emotional. She was also very outspoken, right up front. She would be sitting at the table and say, "Oh, hot flash, hot flash, open the window!" She was open about life and the body—plain-spoken, an unpretentious New Englander. Neither style nor the latest fashion was important to her."

Lady Frances Russell and her grandson Bertrand

—•••••—

On Following Your Own Path

Welsh-born Bertrand Russell was among the most influential philosophers of the twentieth century, known for his work in logic and the analytic approach. His major works included *Principles of Mathematics, Principia Mathematica,* and *Human Knowledge*. A fiercely independent thinker, Russell was controversial throughout his life for antiwar and antinuclear protests.

Orphaned by age four, Bertrand was taken in by his influential grandparents, Lord John Russell (a former prime minister) and Lady Frances. After Lord John died two years later Bertrand was raised almost solely by Frances. In his widely read *Autobiography,* the great philosopher recollected:

My grandmother was the most important person to me throughout my childhood. She was a Scotch Presbyterian, liberal in politics and religion (she became a Unitarian at the age of seventy), but extremely strict in all matters of morality. Of psychology in the modern sense, she had, of course, no vestige. Certain motives were known to exist: love of country, public spirit, love of one's children were laudable motives; love of money, love of power, vanity were bad motives. Good men acted from good motives always; bad men, however, even the worst, had moments when they were not wholly bad. . . .

Her fearlessness, her public spirit, her contempt for convention, and her indifference to the opinion of the majority have always seemed good to me and have impressed themselves upon me as worthy of imitation. She gave me a Bible with her favorite texts written on the fly-leaf. Among these was "Thou shalt not follow a multitude to do evil." Her emphasis upon this text led me in later life to be not afraid of belonging to small minorities.

Natalie Perske and her daughter
Lauren Bacall

●━━━━━━●

On Believing in Yourself

Lauren Bacall was one of Hollywood's leading actresses for several decades. Beautiful, tough talking, and husky voiced, she debuted at the age of nineteen playing opposite Humphrey Bogart in the 1944 movie *To Have and Have Not*. She subsequently married Bogie—who was a quarter century her senior—creating a formidable team on and off screen. Like Greta Garbo and Marlene Dietrich before her Bacall was able to play a wide range of roles successfully, from the wealthy, enigmatic Vivian in *The Big Sleep* to the distraught wife in *Written on the Wind*. After an eight-year hiatus Bacall returned to the screen in 1974 for *Murder on the Orient Express*.

In her autobiography, *By Myself,* the famous actress recalled her childhood:

Mother had her own dreams. She had several beaux. . . . But that was not the heart of her life. She had women friends, bright women, all hard workers, and at least two of them with unfulfilled lives. They had mothers to support—there were no men in their lives, they never expected there would be. Mother did—only she would never settle. No compromise in love a second time. He would be her knight in shining armor or there would be no one.

She always taught me character. That was the most important thing in life. There was right and wrong. You did not lie—you did not steal—you did not cheat. You worked for a living and you worked hard. Accomplishment. Being the best you could be was something to be proud of. You learned the value of a dollar—money was not to be squandered, it was too hard to come by, and you never knew when you might need it. Save for a rainy day (a lesson still unlearned). She had great humor—it was always possible for her to see the funny side. I guess that's how she got through the tough times.

Sidonie Colette and her daughter
Sidonie-Gabrielle

—•••••••—

On Coping Well with Aging

The French writer Sidonie-Gabrielle Colette, known as Colette, stands among the literary giants of the twentieth century. Born in Saint-Sauveur-en-Puisaye, she wrote her early books in collaboration with her first husband, Henry Gauthier-Villars. After their divorce in 1906 she appeared in music halls as a dancer and mime, then settled into full-time writing. Her most famous novels include the semiautobiographical Claudine series, *Cheri,* and *Gigi,* which all vividly portray women in love and jealous affairs.

Even after achieving fame Colette remained very close to her mother, Sido—and cited the following letter, written by Sido in her midseventies, as exemplifying her mother's ability to cope admirably with aging:

Sir,

You ask me to come and spend a week with you, which means I would be near my daughter, whom I adore. You who live with her know how rarely I see her, how much her presence delights me, and I'm touched that you should ask me to come and see her. All the same, I'm not going to accept your kind invitation, for the time being at any rate. The reason is that my pink cactus is probably going to flower. It's a very rare plant I've been given, and I'm told that in our climate, it flowers only once every four years. Now, I am already a very old woman, and if I went away when my pink cactus is about to flower, I am certain I shouldn't see it flower again.

So I beg you, sir, to accept my sincere thanks and my regrets, together with my kind regards.

As a middle-aged woman, Colette commented about her mother's letter in this way:

Whenever I feel myself inferior to everything about me, threatened by my own mediocrity, frightened by the discovery that a muscle is losing its strength, a desire its power, or a pain the keen edge of its bite, I can still hold up my head and say to myself, "I am the daughter of the woman who wrote this letter—that letter and so many more that I have kept.

"This one tells me in ten lines that at the age of seventy-six, she was planning journeys and undertaking them, but that waiting for the possible bursting into bloom of a tropical flower held everything up and silenced even her heart, made for love. . . .

"Let me not forget that I am the daughter of a woman who bent her head, trembling, between the blades of a cactus, her wrinkled face full of ecstasy over the promise of a flower, a woman who herself never ceased to flower, untiringly, during three-quarters of a century."

Glückel of Hameln

On Creating a Balanced Life

A seventeenth-century German Jew from a prominent family, Glückel of Hameln married at fourteen and gave birth to thirteen children. After her husband's death Glückel actively continued his pearl business by attending merchant fairs throughout Germany. She later remarried a wealthy banker in Metz who went bankrupt, leaving her in dire financial straits.

At forty-six Glückel wrote her memoirs as a way to offer her children advice on living wisely and ethically. Among her recommendations:

> I do not intend, my dear children, to compose and write for you a book of morals. Such I could write, and our wise men have already written many. Moreover, we have our holy Torah in which we may find and learn all that we may need for our journey through this world and the world to come. . . .

I pray you this, my children: be patient . . . and the best thing for you is to serve God from your heart without falsehood or deception, not giving out to people that you are one thing while—God forbid—you are in your heart another. Say your prayers with awe and devotion. During the time for prayers, do not stand about and talk of other things. While prayers are being offered to the Creator of the world, hold it a great sin to engage another man in talk about an entirely different matter—shall God Almighty be kept waiting until you have finished your business?

Moreover, set aside a fixed time for the study of the Torah, as best as you know how. Then diligently go about your business, for providing your wife and children with a decent livelihood is likewise a *mitzvah* [good deed], the command of God and the duty of man. We should, I say, put ourselves to great pains for our children, for on this the world is built.

Abigail Kay and her daughter Mary

●━━━━━●

On Developing a Competitive Drive

In mid-1963, after a successful twenty-five-year career in direct sales, Mary Kay Ash retired—for a month. Setting out to write a book to help women survive in the male-dominated business world, she instead developed a business plan for a direct-selling company based on the concept of providing unlimited opportunity for women. Pursuing this dream, she committed her entire life savings of five thousand dollars to launching her new company. With the help of her twenty-one-year-old son, Richard, she launched Mary Kay Cosmetics that September.

Today the company has more than 475,000 independent salespeople, known as beauty consultants, in twenty-six countries worldwide. After her husband, Mel, died of cancer in 1980 Mary became committed to helping find a cure for this disease and was instrumental in the passage of Texas legislation requiring insurance coverage for mammograms.

An active find-raiser for cancer research, she dedicated the Mary Kay Ash Center for Cancer Immunotherapy Research at St. Paul Medical Center in Dallas in 1993. In 1996, the Mary Kay Ash Charitable Foundation was established to fund research on cancers affecting women.

Besides her autobiography, *Mary Kay,* she has authored two other bestsellers, *You Can Have It All* and *Mary Kay on People Management.* In *Mary Kay,* this dynamic entrepreneur reminisced about her early years:

> When I was seven years old, my daddy came from the sanatorium. His tuberculosis had been completely cured in his three years there, and he remained an invalid for the rest of my years at home, in need of a great deal of tender, loving care.
>
> My mother was the sole support of our family for all those years. She managed a restaurant in Houston, and [throughout] my childhood, my mother constantly told me, "Anything anyone else can do, you can do better!" After hearing that enough times, I became convinced that I *could* do better. One of the things she believed I could do was make straight *A's*—*B's* just weren't acceptable. After a while, I didn't want to disappoint my mother or myself. . . .
>
> Of course, I didn't always win. But my mother taught me how to lose. She encouraged me to look to the future: to do better the

next time—to try harder. I think it's important for young people to learn that "you can't win 'em all." Because anyone who competes has to face defeat sooner or later, and learn how to go on from there.

The competitive spirit my mother had instilled in me kept me going through some very difficult days.

Mary Bitnam Davis and her granddaughter Roseanne

◆━━━━━━◆

On Developing Courage

Actress and director Roseanne is best known for the long-running television sitcom that bore her name. Its portrait of working-class life came partly from her own experience: Growing up a Jewish outcast in the strict Mormon society of Salt Lake City, Utah, Roseanne had a difficult time. As a teenager in the 1960s she had a terrifying near-death experience and was placed in a mental institution. She became a mother at an early age and was a member of the working poor. But she never gave up. She succeeded as a stand-up comedian in the 1980s and finally broke through into television, hosting several specials and series and starring in her own show, *Roseanne,* beginning in 1988.

In her first autobiography, *Roseanne: My Life as a Woman,* the popular actress reminisced about her grandmother, nicknamed Bobbe:

[It] happened on Friday night in [Bobbe's] kitchen. My little brother was continually bouncing a ball on the floor, and my father, not known for his tolerance or patience, kept screaming at him to stop it.

Bobbe said to Daddy, "Let him bounce his ball, what does it hurt?" Father, needing to assert himself over the woman who really controlled his wife, his children and his life, said, "He is my kid, I'll tell him what to do, stay out of this. Ben, stop bouncing that ball. Now."

Bobbe began to shake slightly. She said, "He can bounce his ball in my house." Father was uncontrollable at that point, so insulted, so put down that he walked over and hit my little brother.

The tension was unbearable. Bobbe rose, like a Goddess from her red kitchen chair, hobbled over to where my father was standing. . . . and slapped him across the face. Then she spoke. "You do not hit my grandchildren, do you understand?"

This was the first time anyone had ever stood up for us against our father. For a second, he looked at her as if he would kill her. You could see his breath and his wheels churning. She said, "So now you'll beat me, too, huh?" and stood there, defiant, powerful, the birth giver, bread giver. . . .

Father, choking back sobs, said, "Helen, get your coat and the kids, we're never coming back here again." He went out to the car and sat there honking the horn.

Mother did not get up immediately, because Bobbe said, "Let him wait." We all took our time getting on our coats and Bobbe kissed all of us, for a long, slow time. The horn stopped honking, and Mother was, for the first time now, standing up to her husband. As we left, I turned to look at her kiss Bobbe goodbye.

We drove home in silence, and me and my sister Geraldine were elbowing each other in the backseat. We couldn't wait to get home, to go to our room and impersonate Bobbe doing her "Showdown at Park Street." Sometimes, being a daughter is remarkable.

Mary Trump and her son Donald

■■■■■■

On Personal Flair

Born and raised in New York City, "the Donald"—as he is dubbed by the mass media for his headline-grabbing antics—worked closely as a young man with his father, Fred, a residential real estate developer, (whose Trump Organization he eventually took over). Starting in the late 1970s, Trump boldly expanded the organization's holdings and constructed increasingly grandiose buildings, including the hugely profitable Trump Tower, at a time when New York's real estate market seemed in a near-meltdown. His high-profile deal making and enthusiastic self-promotion gained him celebrity status.

Though he crashed into near-bankruptcy in 1990 Trump remains a newsmaking, flamboyant figure, constantly capturing public attention by planning glittering new projects. He is also extremely devoted to his widowed mother, Mary. In his semiautobiography, *The Art of the Deal,* the Donald recalled his formative years:

Looking back, I realize now that I got some of my sense of showmanship from my mother. She always had a flair for the dramatic and the grand. She was a very traditional housewife, but she also had a sense of the world beyond her.

I still remember my mother, who is Scottish by birth, sitting in front of the television set to watch Queen Elizabeth's coronation and not budging for an entire day. She was just enthralled by the pomp and circumstance, the whole idea of royalty and glamour.

I also remember my father that day, pacing around impatiently. "For Christ's sake, Mary," he'd say. "Enough is enough, turn it off. They're all a bunch of con artists." My mother didn't even look up. They were total opposites in that sense. My mother loves splendor and magnificence, while my father, who is very down-to-earth, gets excited only by competence and efficiency.

Pat Nixon and her daughter
Julie

●━━━━━━●

On Having a Sociable Demeanor

Early life was hard for Thelma Catherine Ryan, who acquired her nickname, Pat, within hours of her birth in Nevada. Her Irish father, William, a miner, dubbed her "St. Patrick's babe in the morn" when he arrived home before dawn on March 16, 1912. Soon the family moved to California and settled on a small truck farm near Los Angeles. After the death of her mother, Kate, thirteen-year-old Pat had to assume all household duties for William and two older brothers. At eighteen she lost her father after nursing him through months of illness.

Left on her own, Pat was determined to continue her education. Holding a series of part-time jobs on campus, as a salesclerk in a fashionable department store, and as an extra in the movies, she graduated cum laude from the University of Southern California in 1937. She accepted a position as a schoolteacher in Whittier and there met

Richard Nixon, who had returned home from Duke University Law School to establish a practice; they became acquainted in a little theater group when cast in the same play and were married in June 1940. Throughout her husband's all-consuming political career she was tirelessly supportive while raising two daughters, Tricia and Julie—and once remarked, "It takes heart to be in political life."

In *Pat Nixon, The Untold Story,* Julie Nixon Eisenhower recalled:

Because my father [as Vice President] wanted the few hours he did have with his family to be harmonious, he left all the disciplining to Mother. His severest reprimand was, "I wouldn't do that, honey." Mother's disciplining technique was "the look," as Tricia and I called her freezing, reproachful glance. She did not spank, raise her voice, or whine. If we failed to heed "the look," we had to endure the most dreaded treatment for major offenses: her silence. And because the silence was so impenetrable and such a contrast to the usually loving woman, we avoided provoking it.

To Mother as well went the task of explaining why she, and more often my father, had to be away during a holiday or miss a school or Girl Scout event. Consequently, when she was home, she tried to give us almost one hundred percent of her time. She took us on many outings—the zoo, museums, movies, ice skating. . . .

The Republican Convention was held in Chicago, beginning on July 25 [1960]. Tricia and I had spent most of the month at camp in Montecito, California. A few weeks before we were to fly to Chicago, Mother wrote me and included in her note the injunction, "Keep this letter for instructions." She explained how "a Secret Service friend" would pick up Tricia and me and drive us to our grandmother's house, and when we arrived in Chicago, we would find new dresses that she had hemmed, hoping we had not grown two inches in the past few weeks. She also gave me some advice, which reflected her own philosophy of life:

"In regard to the girls in your cabin [I had complained that some were not friendly]: Just remember that some people are not as friendly and sweet as others. The main thing is to treat them in a friendly fashion and stay your own sweet self, rather than becoming like them. When you think kind thoughts about them, they will change for the better. That is true through life. I love you very, very much!"

Mary, mother of Jesus

On Faith in God

Mary, the mother of Jesus, is presented as a woman of few words. What little we know of her comes mostly from the Gospel of Luke, which attributed to her a prayer known as the Magnificat. Because of its frequent recitation within the Catholic liberation movement, government officials have outlawed this prayer in sections of Latin America today.

Here is its entirety from Luke 1:46–55:

> And Mary said, "My soul magnifies the Lord, and my spirit rejoices in God my Savior, for he has looked with favor on the lowliness of his servant. Surely, from now on all generations will call me blessed; for the Mighty One has done great things for me, and holy is his name. His mercy is for those who fear him generation to generation. He has shown strength with his arm; he has

scattered the proud in the arrogance of their hearts. He has brought down the powerful from their thrones, and lifted up the lowly. He has filled the hungry with good things."

Therese McCarthy and her daughter Mary

———•••••———

On the Privilege of Religion

Mary McCarthy was one of America's foremost literary critics in a career spanning over fifty years. She also wrote novels—including *The Group, Birds of America,* and *Cannibals and Missionaries*—as well as short stories, essays, travel books, and autobiography. Much of her work is satirical, dealing with contemporary issues and events.

Born in Seattle, McCarthy as a youngster moved with her close-knit family to Minneapolis, where her grandparents and other relatives lived. In her popular *Memories of a Catholic Girlhood* the novelist warmly recalled:

> "My mother is a child of Mary," I used to tell other children, in the same bragging spirit that I spoke of my father's height. My mother, not long after her marriage, was converted to Catholicism and though I did not know what a Child of Mary was (actually a member of a sodality of the Ladies of the Sacred

Heart), I knew it was something wonderful from the way my mother spoke of it.

She was proud and happy to be a convert, and her attitude made us feel that it was a special treat to be a Catholic, the crowning treat and privilege. Our religion was a present to us from God. Everything in our home life conspired to fix in our minds the idea that we were very precious little persons, precious to our parents and to God, too, who was listening to us with loving attention every night when we said our prayers.

"It gave you a basic complaisancy," a psychoanalyst once told me (I think he meant "complacency"), but I do not recall feeling smug, exactly. It was, rather, a sense of wondering, grateful privilege. Later, we heard a great deal about having been spoiled by our parents, yet we lacked that discontent that is the real mark of the spoiled child. To us, our existence was perfect, just the way it was.

Anna Russ and her grandson
Leroi Jones (Amiri Baraka)

━━━━━━━

On Trying Again

Based in his hometown of Newark, New Jersey, Baraka has been a prolific author, editor, and publisher on the African-American experience for more than forty years. During the tumultuous "black power" era of the late 1960s, while still known as Leroi Jones, he gained a national audience for his fierce literary denunciation of racist conditions in America's urban areas. In the aftermath of often violent racial riots throughout many northeastern cities, including his native Newark, Jones—who in 1967 became a Muslim and changed his name—helped arouse public concern about black-white tensions outside of the Deep South.

In *The Autobiography of Leroi Jones,* the gifted writer recollected:

It was my grandmother who most times fed us, and her spirit is always with us as a part of our own personalities (I hope). I loved my grandmother so much because she was Good, if that had any meaning in the world. She'd tell you, "Do unto others as you'd have them do unto you," and you knew that's what she believed and that's what she practiced. She'd tell me when I was doing something she approved of, "Practice makes perfect!" Maybe it was being polite, emptying the garbage like I was supposed to, or having shined shoes, or even getting good grades in grammar school. "Practice makes perfect." . . .

If I ever thought seriously about "heaven," it was when Grandmother died, because I wanted her to have that since she believed so strongly. I wrote a poem saying that. I'd been writing for a while when she died. Mostly poems in magazines, and I always regretted that she never got to see a book of mine. I had the dust jacket of *Blues People* in my hand around the time she died, a few weeks later it came out. And I wanted her to see all the dreams and words she'd known me by had some reality, but it was too late. She was gone . . . I wanted my Nana to see that I'd learned "Practice Makes Perfect." But she was gone.

Beatrice Roberts and her daughter
Margaret Thatcher

●●●●●●

On Leading an Active Life

Margaret Thatcher was the first woman to serve as England's prime minister. Born into a middle-class, politically involved family in Lincolnshire, she studied at Oxford University, worked as a research chemist after World War II, then shifted to a career in law and politics while raising two children. She became Conservative Party leader and prime minister in 1975 and for fifteen years politically headed her nation; her three-term tenure marked her as England's longest-serving prime minister in the twentieth century.

Two years after resigning her post due to party infighting about her stringent economic policies, Thatcher was made a life peer by England's royalty. She continues to advance her political views through public speaking, writing, and a private foundation named for her. In her autobiography, *The Path to Power,* Thatcher reminisced about her early life:

When my mother, sister, and I went on holiday together, usually to Skegness, there was also the same emphasis on being active, rather than sitting around day-dreaming. . . .

The loss of my mother, who died in 1960, [produced an] emptiness in my life which could never be filled. She had been a great rock of family stability. She managed the household, stepped in to run the shop when necessary, entertained, supported my father in his public life and as Mayoress, did a great deal of voluntary social work for the church, displayed a series of practical domestic talents such as dressmaking and was never heard to complain. Like many people who live for others, she made possible all that her husband and daughters did.

Her life had not been an easy one. Although in later years, I would speak more readily of my father's political influence on me, it was from my mother that I inherited the ability to organize and combine so many different duties of an active life.

Jane Reno and her daughter Janet

━━━━━━

On Achieving Goals

Janet Reno is the first woman to serve as attorney general of the United States. She was nominated by President Bill Clinton weeks after he first took office and reappointed to her post in early 1997. Raised in Miami, Florida, she was among a handful of women in her class at Harvard Law School; she subsequently returned to south Florida to seek a legal career emphasizing public service. First elected state's attorney in November 1978, Reno was returned to office four more times. Among her accomplishments were the reform of the juvenile justice system, the pursuit of delinquent fathers for child support payments, and the establishment of the Miami Drug Court.

Reno's mother, Jane, raised her children and then became an investigative reporter for the *Miami News*. As Janet Reno's biographer, Paul Anderson, related in *Janet Reno: Doing the Right Thing:*

Of all the women in Janet Reno's life, none had a more profound influence than her hurricane-loving mother. Outspoken, outrageous, absolutely indifferent to others' opinions, Jane Reno was truly one of a kind. . . .

Asked once if she considered herself a feminist, Reno answered, "My mother always told me to do my best, to think my best, and to do right and consider myself a person."

Reno always admired her mother's determination in life. During her confirmation hearings before the Senate Judiciary Committee, she told a hushed audience how [her home] was built in 1948 and 1949, and how much it meant to her.

"There were four children a year apart, and were outgrowing [our previous house]. Daddy didn't have very much money. One afternoon, Mother picked us up at school, and she said, 'I'm going to build a house.' We said, 'What do you know about building a house?' And she said, 'I'm going to learn.'

"And she went and talked to the brickmason and the electrician and plumber, and she learned how to build a house. She dug the foundation with her own hands with a pick and shovel, she laid the bricks, she put in the wiring, she put in the plumbing, and Daddy would help her with the heavy work when he got home from work at night.

"I have lived in that house ever since, and as I come down the driveway through the woods at night, with a problem, with an obstacle to overcome, that house is a symbol to me that you can do anything you really want if it's the right thing to do and you put your mind to it."

Dorothy Rodham and her daughter Hillary

●──●●●●●●

On Being Assertive

As first lady of the United States since Bill Clinton became its forty-second president, Hillary Rodham Clinton has been an icon to many women of her generation. A brilliant study at Wellesley College and then Yale Law School, she served as a staff attorney on the Senate Watergate Committee investigating the Nixon White House before subordinating her own career to that of her husband and helping to raise their child, Chelsea. Over the years of the Clinton administration, Hillary has sought to remain active and influential in American public life—producing the bestseller *It Takes a Village* and speaking out especially on children's issues.

Born in Chicago in 1947, she moved at the age of three with her family to the elm-shaded community of Park Ridge. As biographer Norman King recounted in *The Woman in the White House:*

Hillary did not take very happily to suburban life at first. She was simply unaccustomed to playing with many other children, since there was little chance for extensive socializing in Chicago's apartments. Now she suddenly found herself with other youngsters, and felt frightened by their aggressive and hostile intentions.

One day when Hillary was about four years old, a particularly obnoxious girl started picking on her. The neighbor child was gaining enormous prestige by making the newcomer burst into tears, almost on cue. Hillary sought refuge with her mother in the house.

Dorothy Rodham found her little daughter's fearfulness a new experience. "You can do two things," she advised Hillary. "You can ignore her"—and then she quoted the old maxim, "Sticks and stones may break my bones, but names will never hurt me"—or you can fight back."

Fighting back was a new concept for Hillary, who had never had to fend for herself against her peers. She took her mother's first advice and tried to ignore the girl. When that didn't work, Hillary ran back into her house and sought her mother's solace again.

Dorothy was surprised by her daughter's inability to stand up to her tormentor. "Hillary," she said, "you can stay inside here with me forever, if you want to, or you can go out there and face that kid yourself."

At first, Hillary did nothing. Fighting was something unfamiliar to her. When she had worked herself up to the idea of fighting, Hillary went outside. Positioning herself behind a curtain, Dorothy watched through a window. She saw the tough girl come up to Hillary, punch her in the chest, kick her, and push her down in the street. Dorothy sighed, thinking she would have to devise some other method for helping her daughter.

Then she saw little Hillary crawl to her feet. "Hillary stood up and went after [the other girl] and gave her as good as she got," Dorothy recalled fondly more than forty years later. "It's just an idea we can always refer to—when somebody is beating on us, we go out and take care of things."

Whoopi Goldberg

◆◆◆◆◆◆

On Independence

One of Hollywood's and Broadway's leading actresses, Whoopi Goldberg was born Caryn Johnson in New York City and spent her early years in a drug-ridden housing project. She made her performing debut at age eight with the Helena Rubenstein Children's Theatre at the Hudson Guild. After dropping out of high school, she found work as a summer camp counselor and in the choruses of such 1970s Broadway shows as *Hair, Pippin,* and *Jesus Christ, Superstar*.

Whoopi's film career ignited when director Steven Spielberg cast her in the leading role of *The Color Purple,* based on Alice Walker's novel. She won an Academy Award for the hugely successful movie *Ghost,* and ever since has been a frequent presence on stage, television, and screen. Most recently she starred in the Broadway revival of *A Funny Thing Happened on the Way to the Forum*. Whoopi is also well known for her activism on behalf of many charitable and social organizations, and her openness about her impoverished origins.

In her freewheeling memoir titled simply *Book*, Whoopi Goldberg recounted:

> One night when my [daughter Alex] was maybe thirteen or fourteen, she came downstairs wearing three pieces of cloth. She said she was going out, and it was none of my business where. I looked this child over, this little version of me. The cloth itself was all shiny and nice and fine, but it wasn't covering enough to suit a mother. . . .
>
> Before my mother could come out of my mouth, she was in my ear. I heard her chuckling in the corner, laughing at me over the way our situation had turned. This was parental justice. . . . "Why are you laughing?"
>
> "Because it's funny," she said. "Because it's funny to see you like this now."
>
> Funny? I'm trying to explain to this child that she . . . can't go out looking like this because you don't know what invitation someone is going to pick up from this.
>
> That line—you don't know what invitation someone is going to pick up from this—was one of my mother's, and I wanted to suck it right back into my face as soon as I'd said it. . . . [Then] I wanted to tell my mother how sorry I was for putting her through all those motions, for not recognizing that she had something to offer beyond what I could see. . . .

I turned to my kid and said, "You know what? Go out. Just go."

And she did. She looked at me kinda funny, and suspicious, but she went out like she'd pleased. And then she came back, about twenty minutes later. "You know what?" she asked. "It's cold out there. I think I'm gonna change, put a little more on."

It happens, but it takes time. I watch now as my daughter goes through it herself, with her own kids, and I try not to chuckle. She'll hear me coming out of her mouth and she'll look over with one of those knowing smiles and start to laugh, because we all get it, eventually.

Ollie and Lola Totto and their niece
Georgia O'Keeffe

———————

On Setting an Example

Georgia O'Keeffe, considered one of America's most important modernist painters, is best known for her near-abstract paintings based on enlargements of flower and plant forms—works of great elegance, rhythmic vitality, and sensuousness. Born in rural Wisconsin, O'Keeffe became a member of the photographer Alfred Stieglitz's New York City coterie after meeting him in 1916. They married eight years later. In the 1930s she began spending winters in New Mexico; she settled there permanently after Stieglitz's death in 1946. Thereafter, desert landscapes began to appear prominently in her paintings. O'Keeffe traveled widely in the 1950s, and many of her later works were inspired by views of the earth, sky, and clouds from an airplane.

Maternal figures played a guiding role in O'Keeffe's early life, as revealed in *Georgia O'Keeffe: A Life* by Roxanna Robinson:

Most of Georgia's familial role models were female. . . . Grandmother Totto was a tall and dignified woman with regal bearing and thick white hair. . . .

Ida Totto's sisters Ollie and Lola were strong and frequent presences in Georgia's life. . . . Lola used to visit the O'Keeffes in the summer. Her arrival would be reported in the social notes of the local newspaper, and in August 1897, the paper announced that Miss Lenore Totto had returned to Milwaukee after her stay with the O'Keeffes. "Accompanying her was Miss Georgia O'Keeffe." Visiting the aunts was a great adventure and gave Georgia a new sort of life to consider.

Staying with the two women in the urban environment revealed an alternative to the domestic world her mother had chosen. Aunt Lola, Georgia believed, was a reliable source of all knowledge. Aunt Ollie, a fiercely independent woman, worked for a newspaper and was a source of great family pride.

The women who surrounded Georgia in her early years were strong ones. She was taught, through example, that women were powerful and effective presences, that, single or married, they could live interesting lives . . . full of responsibility and commitment, and equally full of pleasure and gratification.

Caroline Oates and her daughter Joyce

•••••••

On Patience

Joyce Carol Oates has authored more than thirty books, including such novels as *A Garden of Earthly Delights, Unholy Lives,* and *Expensive People*. Her widely published short stories have appeared in collections such as *Last Days* and *Raven's Wing*.

Raised in small-town Lockport, New York, near the Canadian border in the 1940s, Oates was the first of three children. Her parents were not well educated but seem to have created a happy life for their growing family. In an essay paying tribute to her mother's memory, the novelist gratefully recalled in "A Letter to My Mother Caroline Oates on Her 75th Birthday":

> Who taught me patience, if not you? The sometimes-consoling rituals of housekeeping, small simple finite tasks executed with love, or at any rate, bemused affection, cheerful resignation. You

tried to teach me to knit, and to sew, for which feminine activities I demonstrated little talent if, at the outset, energy and hope.

You had more success teaching me to iron, a dreamy mesmerizing task I seem to have liked, as girls will, in small intermittent doses. Though not so much as I came to like vacuuming, a more robust, even acrobatic activity.

And I enjoyed cooking with you, cooking under your easygoing tutelage. Just the two of us, you and me, preparing supper together in the kitchen. This is how you set the timer for the oven. This is how you use the Mixmaster—see the speeds? This is how you whip egg whites. This is how you stir the macaroni to keep it from sticking in the pan. This is how you make a Jell-O mold. This is how you set the table, paper napkins neatly folded in two at the left side of the plates. This is how you smile when you don't especially feel like smiling, this is how you laugh when you don't especially feel like laughing, this is how you prepare a life.

Anna de Mille and her daughter Agnes

◆◆◆◆◆◆

On Making a Good Appearance

If she had been "active in the court of Louis the Fourteenth," wrote designer Oliver Smith, Agnes de Mille "probably would have changed the history of the world." Indeed, Agnes did change the world—of dance. Pioneering a unique American style that combined aspects of modern dance and ballet with a traditional folk idiom, she popularized what had been an elitist art. Her dances for *Oklahoma!, Carousel, Brigadoon,* and other, now classic Broadway shows irrevocably altered American musical theater. Her glittering circle included entertainment figures such as Charlie Chaplin, Noël Coward, Martha Graham, Cole Porter, Richard Rodgers, and Oscar Hammerstein.

Agnes was born into an influential family: Her father was writer-director William, and her uncle was the legendary Hollywood director Cecil B. DeMille. But it was her mother, as biographer Carol Easton astutely observed in *No Intermission: The Life of Agnes de Mille,* who truly shaped Agnes's early life:

Anna was a tiny dynamo; she had considerable charm, the righteousness of a zealot, and the thrift of a miser. Time and money were meant to improve life in some observable way, and to waste either of those precious resources was a sin. "Do something!" was her motto and constant exhortation to her children. . . .

One of Agnes's playmates recalled that, "Anna let you know that there were standards of personal and social behavior that must be maintained—how a well-bred girl should look and behave, what you should read, what you should wear, what you should do for recreation. She had no interest in conventional fashion, only in what she believed to be right. In high school, Agnes suffered from having to wear things like hand-embroidered smocks when her peers were wearing sweaters and skirts. Anna would have a fit if a ribbon wasn't the right color or not in just the right place. To this day, I can hear Anna's voice in the background somewhere, never quite satisfied, saying 'Agnes! You must fix your hair! Must you have this awful disorder! I can't bear to go into your room.'"

Avie Lee and her daughter Dolly Parton

◆◆◆◆◆◆

On Mastering Your Fear

Few country performers have moved from rural roots to international fame more successfully than Dolly Parton. Since her first hit song, "Dumb Blond," in 1967, she has recorded more than sixty albums and sold more than fifty million copies of them worldwide. The Grammy Award–winning singer and songwriter has also starred in such movies as *Nine to Five, Steel Magnolias, The Best Little Whorehouse in Texas,* and *Straight Talk*. Her theme park, Dollywood, annually brings hundreds of thousands of fans to her native eastern Tennessee.

For a woman born into a poor family of twelve children on a run-down farm in Locust Ridge, such achievements are remarkable. In her autobiography, *Dolly, My Life and Other Unfinished Business,* the popular singer reminisced about an inspiration in her childhood:

> My mother had a way of making little games out of things that might be unpleasant or even frightening to us kids. I will never

forget one day at the old house on Locust Ridge. Daddy had gone away for a few days on some kind of trip, and Mama was left back in those woods with all of those kids to tend to. This particular day the sky began to turn yellow, and it looked stormy. I know Mama was worried, but she wouldn't let us know it.

She gathered us all in the house and said we'd play a new game. She had us take the couch and some other furniture and turn it upside down and put it up against the wall. The boys especially liked this part of the game, because they got to do something they would have gotten their butts beat for under normal conditions.

Then Mama said, "Let's all pretend that there's a big storm coming, and let's crawl up under the couch to take cover." Of course, this wasn't pretend at all, but she made us feel like it was. And that kept us from getting too scared.

After a while, it got a lot easier to pretend there was a storm. The wind blew like mad, and we could hear tree limbs snapping and things blowing by the house. Our house was between two mountains, so tornadoes hardly ever came through our little valley. But this one had managed to touch down in our little "holler" like some kind of angry giant sticking out a dark black tongue.

Mama knew it was bad. She said, "Now, let's all pray that the storm will pass over and leave us unharmed." And pray we did. Those of us old enough to know what was really going on prayed like we'd never prayed in our lives.

The noise was horrifying. It sounded like a train was running over our house. After a while, the noise stopped and the wind stopped and we went outside to see what had happened. The storm had done a lot of damage. It had uprooted trees and torn up crops and blown down fences, but our little house had been completely skipped over. If praying really did help, I always thought it must have been Mama's prayers that were actually answered. Hers certainly deserved to be.

Anne Bradstreet

━━━━━━

On Successful Living

Anne Bradstreet was the first important American colonial poet and is best known for her collection *The Tenth Muse Has Lately Sprung Up in America;* much of the book reflects her moral, religious, and scientific outlook. Bradstreet led a leisurely life in Lincolnshire, England, until leaving for the New World at eighteen, already married for two years. Once she arrived she bore eight children and became an active member of Puritan society.

Though articulating a spiritual outlook, Bradstreet opposed the subordinate role women played in Puritan society. In dedicating her book *Meditations Divine and Moral* to her son Simon on March 24, 1664, Bradstreet wrote: "You once desired me to leave something for you in writing that you might look upon, when you should see me no more; I could think of nothing more fit for you nor of more ease to myself than these short meditations." Among her key precepts:

1. There is no object that we see, no action that we do, no good that we enjoy, no evil that we feel or hear, but we may take some spiritual advantage of all; and he that makes such improvement is wise as well as pious.

2. A ship that bears much sail and little or no ballast is easily overset, and that man whose head has great abilities and his heart little or no grace is in danger of foundering.

3. Sweet words are like honey: a little may refresh, but too much gluts the stomach.

4. Diverse children have their different natures; some are like flesh which nothing but salt will keep from putrefaction, some gain like tender fruits that are best preserved with sugar. Those parents are wise that can fit their nurture according to their nature.

5. Authority without wisdom is like a heavy axe without an edge: fitter to bruise than polish.

Lena Roth

●━━●━━●━━●

On Character and Reputation

With its vast opportunities and greater liberty, the United States appealed in the mid- to late-nineteenth century to a growing number of young German Jews seeking a better life. A middle-class woman named Lena Roth offered this useful guidance in 1854 to her son Moses just before her son set sail:

> Although your dear father has already told you everything [that] can be recommended to a young lad of your age and I hope that you will adhere as much as possible to this writing, I cannot abstain to admonish you—that you be content and patient whenever you may not achieve what you had aimed for. It happens to everybody in life once in a while, and you cannot anticipate it. In such a case, you must be very patient, even if it costs you much effort to endure it.

I will [also] recommend one more point that you should keep in mind especially: don't miscalculate ever your own character, especially against other persons who are less worthy than you are yourself. Never act against your own character, be it against men or women. I do not mean those who are poorer than you are, because poor people are many times just as honest as the richest. When a person is honest and righteous, he is just as esteemed as people of rank, but I mean this in quite a different sense. You will understand me—even if not at present—but later, when you have matured.

The main thing is, you must try to keep up your good reputation, since, once you are despised and in bad memory, you stay there forever.

Minnie Sinclair and her grandson Dave Thomas

——————

On Life Lessons

Dave Thomas was easily recognizable for his frequent television commercial appearances as founder of the Wendy's fast-food restaurant chain. He was also an active philanthropist who supported a variety of hospitals and medical research programs. And in 1990 he became a national spokesperson for a White House initiative called Adoption Works . . . for Everyone; he also headed the Dave Thomas Foundation for Adoption.

Born in Atlantic City, Thomas never knew his birth parents, but Rex and Auleva Thomas of Kalamazoo, Michigan, adopted him as a baby. Auleva died when he was five, and Dave's early years included numerous moves as his adoptive father sought work during the Depression.

In his autobiography, *Dave's Way,* the entrepreneur devoted considerable attention to his hardworking grandmother Minnie's inspiring influence on his life, and included this section, titled "Gramma Minnie's Lessons for Living":

1. Make a lot out of a little. Don't waste. Be smart the way you use your time. Do your work in a dependable way.

2. Work hard, and you won't feel so sorry for yourself: Don't sit around and mope. Attend to business. Go out and get something done.

3. Don't cut corners, or you'll sacrifice quality. If you lose quality, you lose everything else. People want to get back the quality they've seen lost in the things they buy.

4. Have fun doing things. Decide how you'll divide your time. When you're having fun, focus on having fun. Learn to enjoy your work as much as you can.

5. Be strict but caring, too. Let people know you have values. Let people know you care about them, too.

6. Tackle problems head-on. Don't run away from challenges. Let people know you're going to hang on until something is solved.

7. Pray.

Maria Lewis and her pupil George Eliot (Mary Ann Evans)

❧❧❧❧❧❧

On Overcoming Adversity

George Eliot was the pen name of Mary Ann Evans, one of England's great nineteenth-century writers. *Silas Marner* and *Middlemarch* are her most famous novels, reflecting her middle-class, rural childhood and youth. Though writing seriously about moral and social problems of her time, Eliot created memorable characters as well.

Eliot's own adolescence was marked by pain and inner struggle. As biographer Tim Taylor related in *A Woman of Contradictions: The Life of George Eliot:*

> After the death of her mother from cancer when Mary Ann was sixteen in 1836, she fell into a long period of withdrawal and depression. Mary Ann longed for her mother's companionship. Also, the death required her to manage household chores, rather

than enroll in a progressive boarding-school in Manchester. Mary Ann's demanding father and brother saw her becoming increasingly sad and self-pitying. But they insisted on her domestic role.... Then, in 1838, Mary Ann's former teacher Maria Lewis came to serve as her private tutor.

Immediately, Lewis pointed out that matters could be far worse for Mary Ann; at least, she had a warm, comfortable house provided for her—and she did not have to teach pupils who despised her and wished to make her life miserable. When Mary Ann protested that she had no purpose to her existence, Maria countered that in reality, she had received a God-given opportunity to humble herself in service of others. Mary Ann should try to "emulate the character of a Christian who professes to do all, even the most trifling duty, as to the Lord demands." Then she would find a purpose in life.

This advice was instrumental in uplifting Mary Ann's outlook. "God is best served by diligence in all occupations" became her new maxim, enabling her to settle to the intricacies of hiring servants and to set jam with a more hopeful attitude about the future. Thanks to the aid of supportive Maria Lewis, the future "George Eliot" gained a vital sense of direction and esteem in her life.

Eleanor Roosevelt and her daughter Anna

●━●━●━●━●━●

On Facing Difficulty

Eleanor Roosevelt was respected not merely as the wife of President Franklin D. Roosevelt during America's darkest period but also as a distinguished public figure in her own right. She was probably the most active first lady in U.S. history, as well as serving as a delegate to the newly formed United Nations after World War II and chairperson of its Human Rights Commission.

A role model for women as a lecturer, writer, and social activist, Eleanor was also a devoted mother. In August 1948 she offered this heartfelt advice to her daughter, Anna, who had just learned that her teenage son had been stricken with polio:

> Wire me when you hear just how far things extend with "Buzz" [Curtis]. What I hope is that with a light case, involvement of any muscles may be temporary.

Perhaps when things like this happen which seem just too much to bear, we are being given a lesson in values. There is no use trying to teach the weak, but the strong are worth training. When a child is ill, you know that the other losses were of little importance. His life and happiness are all that counts. You work to repay money losses to others because you have a sense of integrity and responsibility. You work for some future security, so as not to be a burden on the young, but you learn that the satisfactions that come are in doing the work well and in making those you love happy.

You are one of the strong people in the world, and I love you dearly.

Agnes Meyer and her daughter
Katherine Graham

●━━●━━●━━●

On Perseverance

The daughter of a Wall Street tycoon and a Washington power broker, Katherine Graham was raised by one of the most politically influential families of the twentieth century. From the day her father bought the *Washington Post* in 1933, her life was marked, and sometimes scarred, by the ups and downs of politics in Washington, D.C. After her husband, Phil Graham's, suicide in 1963, Katherine was suddenly faced with publishing the *Post* herself. Despite an awkward start, she went on to publish the Pentagon Papers and allow reporters Woodward and Bernstein to crack open the Watergate scandal that led to President Nixon's resignation.

Katherine Graham was a bestselling author, preeminent Capitol Hill hostess, and—according to some Washington insiders—among the most powerful women in the world.

In her autobiography, *Personal History,* Graham recalled that her mother enjoyed taking the family on frequent camping trips, seeing these excursions "as bringing us closer to the realities of life and making us more independent." In the summer of 1936, Katherine happily accompanied her parents and siblings on a camping trip to the Canadian Rockies:

We children and our guides caught fish, and my father caught colds. Mother kept a brief diary of the expedition, too, and the following excerpt represents an aspect of her philosophy that she [gave] us:

The fatigue of the climb was great, but it is interesting to learn once more how much further one can go on one's second wind. I think that it is an important lesson for everyone to learn, for it should also be applied to one's mental efforts.

Most people go through life without ever discovering the existence of that whole field of endeavor which we describe as second wind. Whether mentally or physically occupied, most people give up at the first appearance of exhaustion. Thus, they never learn the glory and the exhilaration of genuine effort.

Anne Hamill and her son Pete

•••••••

On Rejecting Prejudice

Pete Hamill is one of America's best-known journalists. Born in 1935 in Brooklyn, New York, to Irish immigrants, Hamill served in the U.S. Navy and attended Mexico City College, Pratt Institute, and the School of Visual Arts. He began his journalistic career with the *New York Post* in 1960, and by 1965 was a regular columnist who had distinguished himself with hard-hitting articles that probed such social problems as urban poverty, racial tensions, and the anti–Vietnam War movement. He was close to Robert F. Kennedy during his 1968 bid for the presidency. Later Hamill worked as a columnist for the *Daily News* and completed several hitches with the *Village Voice;* he was also a contributing editor at the *New York Times Magazine* for twenty-five years.

As a novelist and playwright, Hamill has always concerned himself with the oppressed and downtrodden. In his bestseller *A Drinking Life: A Memoir,* Hamill recalled a childhood conversation with his mother that shaped his outlook:

[S]he was unhappy as she told me about Belfast (on that day, and many others). The city was divided between Catholics like us and Protestants, who were a different kind of Christian.

And though she knew some decent Protestants, in Belfast most of them were bigots. She was a little girl in Belfast when the Troubles started and the bigots formed into the Mother Gang. . . . The British army was there too, with armored cars and machine guns, terrible men who hated the Irish and hated the Catholics. All of that was in Belfast, where the bigots ran everything.

This was at once scary and thrilling, and I made her tell me the stories many times. My mother seemed to me an amazing woman, someone who had seen things when she was a little girl that were more terrible than any movie. And here she was. Smiling. Whistling when she was happy. Telling me that she loved America for its freedom.

Freedom is a lot more important than money, she said. Remember that. Here, we're free. And you must never be a bigot.

What is a bigot, anyway?

A bigot is a hater, she said. A bigot hates Catholics. A bigot hates Jews. A bigot hates colored people. It's no sin to be poor, she said. It is a sin to be a bigot. Don't ever be one of them.

No, Mommy, I said. I won't be one of them.

Abby Aldrich Rockefeller

•••••••

On Standing for Fairness

Abby Aldrich was the buoyant, impulsive daughter of Rhode Island's Senator Nelson Aldrich when, in 1894, she met John D. Rockefeller Jr., the awesomely reserved heir to the Standard Oil fortune. This unlikely pair fell in love, but it was seven years before John felt confident enough to propose. "She was so gay and young and so in love with everything," he later recalled in *Abby Aldrich Rockefeller: The Woman in the Family* by Bernice Kert, "that I kept wondering why she would ever marry a man like me."

But Abby did marry him, in 1901, and her intuitive understanding of people, willingness to experiment, and defiant optimism became the leavening in John's narrow, bureaucratic way of thinking. While raising five children she expanded his vision of what the Rockefeller fortune could do, shaping the family into the progressive force in philanthropy and the arts that we know today.

In February 1923 Abby Aldrich Rockefeller offered her three older teenage sons—John D. III, Nelson, and Laurance—this far-seeing advice:

> For a long time, I have had very much on my mind and heart a certain subject. . . . Out of my experience and observation has grown the conviction that one of the greatest causes of evil in the world is race hatred or race prejudice; in other words, the feeling of dislike that a person or a nation has against another person or nation without just reason, an unreasoning aversion. The two people . . . who suffer most in this country from this kind of treatment are the Jews and the Negroes.
>
> In Europe it is different. The French hate the Italians who in turn hate the Austrians, until in the Balkans every country hates every other country and they all hate the Turks, so it goes on in a "vicious circle."
>
> You boys are still young. No group of people have done you personal injury. I want to make an appeal to your sense of fair play, to begin your lives by giving the other fellow a fair chance and a square deal. It is to the everlasting disgrace of the United States that horrible lynchings and brutal race riots frequently occur in our midst. The social ostracism of the Jews is less barbaric, but causes cruel injustice. I long to have our family stand firmly for what is best and highest in life. If you older boys will do it, the younger will follow.

Dora Birnbaum and her son George Burns

•••••••

On Teaching Faith

For his incredible longevity as well as his unique acting talent, George Burns was recognized as one of America's greatest comedians. The wry, cigar-smoking jokester who played straight man to Gracie Allen for thirty-five years, then found new popularity after winning an Academy Award at age eighty, died only weeks after turning one hundred. For over ninety years, his career spanned turn-of-the-century vaudeville, radio, movies, television, nightclubs, bestselling books, recordings, and videos.

As the Supreme Being in the *Oh, God!* film series during the 1970s and 1980s, Burns wore baggy pants, sneakers, and a golf cap. He said in the article "Thanks for Making Me laugh, Mr. Burns," Waite's Web-World George Burns tribute, he was a bit nervous at first about taking the role, "because I didn't know what kind of makeup He uses." But Burns decided to take the role after reasoning, "Why shouldn't I play God? Anything I do at my age is a miracle." Celebrating his ninety-eighth birthday in Las Vegas, Burns quipped, "It's nice to be here. At ninety-eight, it's nice to be anywhere."

In his final book, *One Hundred Years, One Hundred Stories,* Burns fondly recalled:

Unlike my father, my mother was a very practical lady. Nothing ever flustered her. No matter what the problem was, somehow she knew how to handle it.

A perfect example happened when I was seven years old. I was singing with three other Jewish kids from the neighborhood. We called ourselves the Peewee Quartet. Now, there was a big department store, Siegel & Copper, that threw an annual picnic, and the highlight was an amateur contest with talent representing all the churches in New York. Right around the corner from where we lived was a Presbyterian church. How it got into that neighborhood, I'll never know; it certainly didn't do big business.

Well, they had no one to enter in the contest, so the minister asked us four kids to represent the church. We jumped at the chance. So that Sunday, there we were: the Peewee Quartet— four Jewish kids sponsored by a Presbyterian church—and our opening song was "When Irish Eyes Are Smiling." We followed that with "Mother Machree" and won first prize. The church got a purple velvet altar cloth, and each of us kids got an Ingersoll watch, which was worth about eighty-five cents.

Well, I was so excited I ran all the way home to tell my mother. When I got there she was on the roof hanging out the wash. I rushed up to her and said "Mama, I don't want to be a Jew anymore!"

If this shocked her, she certainly didn't show it. She just looked at me and calmly said, "Do you mind me asking why?"

I said, "Well, I've been a Jew for seven years and never got anything. I was a Presbyterian for one day and I got a watch." And I held out my wrist and showed it to her.

She glanced at it and said, "First help me hang up the wash, then you can be a Presbyterian."

While I was hanging up the wash some water ran down my arm and got inside the watch. It stopped running, so I became a Jew again.

Dorothy Walker Bush and her son George

———

On Humility

Throughout his early life and ensuing political career culminating as the forty-first U.S. president, George Bush viewed his mother as inspirational for her dynamism and confidence in his abilities.

A favorite family anecdote was related in *George Bush: The Life of a Lone Star Yankee* by Herbert Parmet. It involved Dorothy's first pregnancy. Although in her ninth month, with Prescott Bush Jr. on the way, she was playing in one of the usual family softball games behind their summer house in Kennebunkport, Maine. As her children always enjoyed recounting, Dorothy hit a home run on her last time at bat, ran around the bases to score her run, and then shouted, "I'm in labor. Let's go to the hospital!" On that same day, her first child was born.

Dorothy was revered by her children for her characteristic disdain for self-importance, a trait she worked to pass on to her children. Once, when George told her that he had lost a tennis match because his game had been off, she responded with, "You don't have a game." Even much later, she monitored his manners and display of ego. When he was vice president, she admonished him for bad manners when he appeared to be reading while President Reagan was giving a speech, rejecting his explanation that he was merely following the printed text. George himself told some of those around him about her complaints that he tended to "talk about himself too much."

At the age of ninety-one, Dorothy Bush died a few days after the 1992 Presidential election. By her deathbed, George found a frayed Bible and letters he had written as a teenager to her from Andover. "She was the beacon in our family—the center, the candle around which all the moths fluttered—she was there, the strength, the power but never arrogance, just love was her strength, kindness, her main virtue. How many times she taught us to be kind to the other guy, never hurt feelings, love."

Betty Shabazz

⬥⬥⬥⬥⬥⬥

The Value of Community

The famous widow of Malcolm X, tragically killed in a fire set by her disturbed grandson in June 1997, had a tumultuous life. Raised in Detroit and attending the Tuskegee Institute, Betty Shabazz became a registered nurse and married Malcolm in 1958 when he was a minister of Harlem's Mosque No. 7. It was seven years later that, pregnant with twins, she was in the audience with their four other children when gunmen shot and killed Malcolm X as he preached onstage. Her nursing training proved fruitless as she rushed to Malcolm's bullet-riddled body and sobbed, "They killed him."

A model of strength, courage, and dignity, Shabazz went on to earn a doctoral degree in education and become a university administrator. As a spokesperson for civil rights, she raised her six children alone while subjected to media scrutiny. Later, Dr. Shabazz served as director of public relations at Medgar Evers College in Brooklyn, New

York, and also headed its Office of Institutional Advancement. In an interview with *Upscale* magazine published a month before her death, Dr. Shabazz offered her viewpoint on teaching children to create genuine community:

> I think that one of the things that we need to make sure of in this society is that our young people . . . know all individuals have a right to this planet, and that God loves everyone.
>
> Children need to know, too, that their parents love them, and that their community truly cares. If kids fail to get that message, then we have only ourselves to blame.
>
> It is extremely important that we understand that we have a responsibility for the deterioration that we see, and for the ultimate demise of young people and adults. A lot of people sit back and they complain about the politicians, and they complain about the religious leaders, and they complain about this group. But all of us have to accept the responsibility. And, if all of us did our part, then it would not rest so heavily on the shoulders of the few.

Dorothy Williams and her daughter Lynna

━━━━━━

On the Importance of Discretion

Lynna Williams is an associate professor of English and creative writing at Emory University in Atlanta. The author of *Things Not Seen and Other Stories* and a former newspaper reporter and political speechwriter, she grew up in post–World War II Texas. In an essay titled "Everything I Know," Lynna recalled her mother's influence on her writing style and broader character:

> A year of speech therapy before first grade shaped me up, and the family legend goes, I haven't shut my mouth for five minutes since then. Which is why, I suppose, that all the while you were teaching me the fundamental rules of decent living: Sit with your legs together, don't wear rayons in summer, don't use *language;* the stinkier the gift, the sweeter the thank-you note.
>
> It seemed to me that what you wanted me to learn above all was this: *You don't have to tell everything you know*. I can't count

the number of times you said that to me when I was growing up. You were talking, I know now, about discretion, and privacy, and circumspection. All fine things ... so the stories I told you depended on facts, on literal event, on who, what, where, and why. A lifetime later, when I was learning to write fiction instead of newspaper stories, I figured out that it was your house where I learned [this craft].

Lucille Ball and her daughter Lucie Arnaz

❮❮❮❮❮❮❮

On the Gift of Humor

Lucille Ball was one of America's most popular actresses for more than fifty years. Her career began in stage dancing; she then moved on to film. Using her comedic talent in such television programs as *I Love Lucy, Here's Lucy,* and *The Lucy Show,* she shattered many stereotypes about femininity and "ladylike behavior": Countless sitcom episodes showed her scheming to outwit her controlling husband, Ricky, and achieve her goals. It's no accident that Lucille Ball became the first woman in America to own a major entertainment studio, Desilu Productions. Yet playfulness was always vital to her character.

In the foreword to her mother's posthumously published autobiography, *Love, Lucy,* the actress's daughter, Lucie Arnaz, fondly recalled:

> One of my mother's favorite things to do, when a small group of people were involved in some ordinary conversation, was to wait until one of them left the room and as soon as she returned,

blurt out, convincingly, "Here she is now! Why don't we tell her to her face?!!"

This was always followed by frozen silence, and then she'd howl (with that depth-of-the-sea laugh she had) to see the look on the poor soul's face, who for one horrible moment thought someone had been saying terrible things about her while she was gone.

I'm not sure why, but I keep thinking about that now as I sit down to introduce you to this treasure . . . my mother's story of her life.

Loving

Diana, Princess of Wales

•-•-•-•-•-•

On Concern for Others

In her short, tumultuous life Diana, Princess of Wales, came to be one of the world's most popular and admired women. Though bright and attractive, she suffered from low self-esteem from an early age. Only recently, just before her tragic automobile accident in August 1997, did the princess seem to develop a comfortable confidence in herself and her mission in life.

Though her marriage to Prince Charles was marked by unhappiness and even despair, Diana never allowed such difficulties to interfere with her vital role in raising her sons, Harry and William. As biographer Andrew Morton recently related in his book *Diana, Her True Story*:

> The Princess was anxious that her sons should see something of the real world beyond boarding school and palaces. As she said

in a speech on AIDS, "I am only too aware of the temptation of avoiding harsh reality; not just for myself but for my children, too. Am I doing them a favor if I hide suffering and unpleasantness from them until the last possible minute? The last minutes which I choose for them may be too late. I can only face them with a choice based on what I know. The rest is up to them."

She felt this was especially important for William, the future King. As she once said, "Through learning what I do, and his father to a certain extent, he has got an insight into what's coming his way. He's not hidden upstairs with the governess."

Over the years, [Diana] has taken both boys on visits to hostels for the homeless and to see seriously ill people in hospital. When she took William on a secret visit to the Passage day care center for the homeless in Central London, accompanied by Cardinal Basil Hume, her pride was evident as she introduced him to what many would consider the flotsam and jetsam of society.

"He loves it and that is what really rattles people," she proudly told friends. The Catholic Primate of All England was equally effusive. "What an extraordinary child," he told her. "He has such dignity at such a young age." . . .

Again during one ascot week, a time of Champagne, smoked salmon and fashionable frivolity for High Society, the Princess took her boys to the Refuge night shelter for down-and-outs. William played chess while Harry joined in a card school. Two hours later, the boys were on their way back to Kensington Palace, a little older and a little wiser.

"They have a knowledge," [Diana] once said. "They may never use it, but the seed is there, and I hope it will grow because knowledge is power. I want them to have an understanding of people's emotions, people's insecurities, people's distress and people's hopes and dreams."

Rachel Boak and her granddaughter
Willa Cather

●━━●━━●━━●━━●━━●

On Caring for Others

A celebrated author of books about midwestern prairie life, Willa Cather was born on a farm near Winchester, Virginia, in 1873. At the age of nine she moved with her family to Nebraska; she lived in that state, where many of her novels are set, until completing college. Cather worked for several years as a journalist, high-ranking magazine editor, and teacher before devoting herself full time to writing at age thirty-nine. Her many novels include *O Pioneers, Death Comes for the Archbishop, My Antonia,* and *One of Ours* (which won a Pulitzer Prize).

Shortly after completing college Cather published an article titled "Nursing as Profession for Women" in which she fondly recalled:

My own grandmother was one of those unprofessional nurses who served without recompense, from the mere love of it, even though she had a host of little children to care for. But you have had grandmothers of your own, so you know how it went. You remember the old woman who nursed you when you had scarlet fever, and walked the floor with you when you had whooping cough. Money will never buy such attendance for you again.

[My grandmother] was the unofficial nurse for Back Creek residents as well as for my own family, risking her own life to help the sick and comfort the dying. Although she had cares enough of her own, poor woman, when a child was burned, when some overworked woman was in her death agony, when a man had been crushed under the falling timber, or when a boy had cut his leg by a slip of the knife in the sumach field, the man who went to town for the doctor always stopped for her on the way.

In *Emerging Voice* by Sharon O'Brien, she states, "Rachel Boak left no written texts that librarians have preserved. Yet Cather gave this grandmother the fullest, most affectionate portrait of a family member in her fiction; she was the model for self-denying grandmother and the strong-willed, compassionate woman."

Christine de Pisan

On Charitable Behavior

Born in Venice, Christine de Pisan (1365–c. 1429) moved as a child to France, where she married at age fifteen. Within a decade she was left a widow with three children, her mother, and a niece to support. They survived as a result of Christine's becoming the first—and only—female professional writer of the Renaissance.

Self-taught and widely read, Christine de Pisan focused on moral issues and the practicalities of daily life. The following excerpt is from *The Treasure of the City of Ladies* (the sequel to *The City of the Ladies*):

> And so, when the princess or great lady practices charity, she acquires greater merit than a lesser woman would in the same situation, for three principal reasons. The first is that the greater the person is and the more she humbles herself, the more her goodness increases. The second is that she gives greater aid and comfort to the poor, as has already been said. And the third, which is

by no means an unimportant reason, is that she gives a good example to those who see her perform such work and with such great humility, for nothing influences the common people so much as what they see their lord and lady do. Therefore, it is a great benefit when lords and ladies and all other persons who hold positions of authority over others are well brought up, and great mischief when they are not. . . .

The noble practice of charity will envelop the heart of the good princess, will render her of such very good will towards all people that she will imagine that everyone is more worthy than she. Since her heart will rejoice as much at the well-being of another as at her own, she will be delighted to hear good reports about other people. To the best of her abilities, in all things she will give opportunities to the good to persevere and to the bad to reform.

Louisa Fuller and her grandson
Andrew Young

·-·-·-·-·-·

On Giving to the Needy

Andrew Young's career as a civil rights activist and public official has spanned nearly forty years. Raised in New Orleans, he became a minister and in 1960 joined the Southern Christian Leadership Conference spearheaded by Dr. Martin Luther King Jr. The two worked together closely, and as the group's executive director from 1964 to 1970 Young took an active role in ending segregation throughout the South. Shortly thereafter he became the first African American to represent Georgia in Congress since 1871 and served under President Jimmy Carter as U.S. representative to the United Nations. Mayor of Atlanta for eight years, Young remains a national figure within the African-American community.

In his semiautobiography, *An Easy Burden: The Civil Rights Movement and the Transformation of America,* Young reminisced about his maternal grandmother and her crucial influence on his life:

My grandmother raised eight children of her own and informally adopted several others [and] I always associated my family's openness, their willingness to help others in need, with Gran's and my parents' strong religious faith. It was a living faith that guided every aspect of their lives.

Gran had a reputation in the neighborhood for feeding people who came to our door hungry. She would feed anybody. Beggars and hoboes, many of whom had just arrived in the city on the railroads . . . apparently passed the word among themselves that if you were really desperate, you could go to 2224 Cleveland Avenue, where some friendly colored people lived, ask for a light-skinned woman named Mrs. Fuller, and most likely get something to eat, even if it was only a slice of French bread and butter.

Feeding the needy seemed to be my grandmother's self-appointed task, and she was never happier than when acting as great-mother-of-the-lost. There were a number of people like that in New Orleans when I was a child—helping the needy had not yet completely institutionalized—and those who volunteered themselves did so with no fear that they would be victimized or taken advantage of.

Vanessa Bell

❧❧❧❧❧❧

On Encouraging Adult Children

The older sister of writer Virginia Woolf, Vanessa Bell was a well-known painter and a major figure in London's iconoclastic "Bloomsbury" circle of writers, artists, and social critics. She studied at the Painting School of the Royal Academy. Along with the art critic Roger Fry and the painter Duncan Grant, Bell founded the celebrated Omega Workshops, which brought a bright, innovative palette to the field of interior design.

Strong, free willed, and passionate, Bell had many romances over the course of her life yet remained a devoted mother to her three children. While painting in Rome in 1935, Vanessa Bell often wrote to her son Julian back in England. Her letters included these encouraging sentiments:

> I was very glad of your nice long letter. You seem to be leading
> a very stimulating life with a good many agitations and ups and

downs of all kinds. Never mind. As long as you're doing things it really interests you to do, I feel it's the main thing, and I'm sure all these curious editorial and other works will give you a lot of very useful experience and friends and reputations, which will eventually lead to your finding out just what you really want to do, and doing it.

You sounded very exhausted in your last letter, my dear. I don't believe writing really takes more out of one than painting, but it seems so, because it's all to do with life, I think, whereas in painting one seems to get into another world altogether, separate from the ordinary human emotions and ideas. Perhaps that's only an illusion, however. But it may be an illusion that helps. It seems such a relief to have this world to plunge into. How I should like to see what you've written.

Rebekah Johnson and her son Lyndon

◆◆◆◆◆◆◆

On Reinforcing Effort

The thirty-sixth president of the United States grew up in small-town Texas. Lyndon Johnson's father was initially a successful and much-admired state politician, but the family sank into near-poverty in the poor business conditions of the mid-1920s. The oldest of five, Lyndon was active and bright but resisted studying. It was his culturally oriented mother, Rebekah, who read him stories from the Bible, history, and mythology and taught him the alphabet when he was two.

As told in *Lone Star Rising* by Robert Dallek:

> In the opinion of many people who observed their interaction over the years, Rebekah had an extraordinary hold on Lyndon; she imbued him with the belief that he could do anything, that nothing was too hard for him. "I think except for her I might not have made it through high school and certainly not through col-

lege. . . . She was a constant, dogged, determined influence on my life."

The evidence of her impact on Lyndon is even more striking from the words they exchanged when he was an adolescent and a man. "You can't realize the difference in the atmosphere after one of your sweet letters," he wrote her early in his college career. "Your letters always give me more strength, renewed courage, and that bulldog tenacity so essential to the success of any man," he wrote at the age of twenty-one.

"I love; I believe in you; I expect great things of you," Rebekah wrote her son when he was twenty-nine. "You have always justified my expectations, my hopes, my dreams. How dear to me you are, my darling boy, my devoted son, my strength and comfort."

Replying to another one of Rebekah's encouraging messages a year later, Lyndon wrote: "Your thoughtful letter . . . I shall remember when I get downhearted and feel like tossing everything out the window. During the years, your letters have meant more to me than I can say. They have urged me on, even when I have despaired of accomplishing anything."

Margaret Mead and her daughter
Mary Catherine Bateson

●━━●━━●━━●

On Feeling Comfortable in the Body

Margaret Mead, an influential anthropologist, was also the first prominent woman in the field. Her most important—and still controversial—books include *Coming of Age in Samoa, Growing Up in New Guinea,* and *Culture and Commitment.* Mead wrote prolifically on cross-cultural topics such as child rearing, marriage, and intimacy, and was named mother of the year by *Time* magazine in 1969. She taught at Columbia University and also served as a curator for the American Museum of Natural History for many decades.

After several miscarriages Mead was told by doctors that she could never bear children. But in 1939 she gave birth to a daughter, Mary Catherine. In her fascinating memoir, *With a Daughter's Eye,* Mead's only child recalled her famous mother's guidance:

Margaret ... was determined that I should grow up with a feeling of friendliness toward my body, and particularly that I should have no negative feelings about menstruation. Margaret was convinced that whole populations do not suffer from dysmenorrhea, or at least that in some groups, the physical sensations associated with the beginning of a menstrual period are not normally identified as discomfort. ... Then, I remember a day of sunshine somewhere in the country of Australia, with that lovely feeling of lightness that often comes two or three days into a menstrual period, and I skipped through a garden, saying how happy I felt, and she talked about feeling a possibility of love and birth and growth, as all kinds of giving, and about feeling a communion with nature in shared biological processes. ...

The moment remains in my memory and there seems to be a direct connection between what she said then and [my] conviction that the menstrual cycle as experienced by women—and, secondhand, by men—might be one of the things that can shape our consciousness toward a sensitivity to the rhythms of natural systems.

Daisy Ellington and her son
Edward ("Duke")

•••••••

On Fostering Self-Esteem

Nicknamed by a boyhood friend who admired his regal air, Duke Ellington is now indelibly associated with the finest creations in American big band and vocal jazz. Over a fifty-year career, Ellington showed a genius for instrumental combinations, improvisation, and jazz arrangement. In 1923 the pianist Fats Waller encouraged him to move to New York City, where during Duke's formative years at Harlem's famous Cotton Club he developed the unique style—evidenced in works such as "Mood Indigo" and "Sophisticated Lady"—that brought him worldwide acclaim.

As highlighted by biographer John Hasse in *Beyond Category: The Life and Genius of Duke Ellington*, Duke's mother, Daisy, exerted a strong influence upon him:

Born in 1879 in Washington, D.C., [she] had come from a middle-class family and completed high-school, a remarkable achievement at the time. Her father had been a District of Columbia police officer, a coveted job for a black man in those days.

Daisy raised young Edward with love, praise, and encouragement. She always treated him as someone very special, telling him, "Edward, you are blessed." Young Edward would maintain this confident feeling of being favored for the rest of his life. Daisy regarded him as her jewel, and when he was stricken with pneumonia, she refused to leave his bedside.

Daisy was also a key influence on her son's future career as musician and bandleader. Like her husband, James, Daisy played the piano, particularly enjoying parlor songs and ragtime pieces. One of Duke's earliest memories was of his mother praying the Rosary so beautifully that "I burst out crying," said Ellington. As a small boy, then, Duke learned that music could evoke strong feelings and provide spiritual uplift.

As Duke's younger sister, Ruth, recalled late in life, "[Edward] said that when he was a little boy and sitting on his mother's lap, he looked into her face and he knew that she was the most beautiful mother in the world. And he felt that way about her until the day she died."

Gabrielle Kerouac and her son Jack

●●●●●●

On Finding Your Way

Jack Kerouac was one of America's most influential writers in the 1950s and 1960s. A hero of the beatnik and hippie movements, he celebrated free-spirited individuality, spontaneous living, and material simplicity in such novels as *On the Road* and *The Dharma Bums*. Growing up in a French-Canadian family in working-class Lowell, Massachusetts, Kerouac won a football scholarship to Columbia University but began experiencing emotional turmoil when his father sank into alcoholism and gambling after failing in business. Disillusioned and confused, Jack quit school and enlisted in the navy, but had problems there, too.

In May 1943 Jack was in basic training when he received these encouraging words from his mother:

> Tell me, honey, what seems to be all the fuss out there? At first
> I thought you were sick, but now Pop tells me you refuse to go

through the training, or in other words, refuse to serve your country. Oh honey *lamb*. That's not like you. Don't you know that it will be an awful mark against you?

You have good education, seems to me you could have done something really good. The Navy is grand, too . . . I don't know what to advise outside of asking you to give it a "fair try."

I suppose I'll be seeing you soon, and when you come, I'll have lots of things to tell you—not fit to write here—so until then, lots of courage, honey, and think carefully. As for me, whatever you do, I won't criticize your judgments. After all, your life's your own. But be brave and tell me all about everything.

Antonetta Ferraro and her daughter Geraldine

●●●●●●●

On Self-Respect

In 1984 Geraldine Ferraro—as Walter Mondale's running mate—became the first woman in U.S. history to be selected a vice presidential candidate by a major political party. With a law background, she had been serving in Congress as a representative of Queens, New York; earlier, she had worked as assistant district attorney for the same Queens area, and also headed a special bureau for victims of violent crime. In 1992 Ferraro ran in the New York senatorial primary but lost the Democratic nomination despite considerable support. In her autobiography, *My Story,* Ferraro recollected:

> Soon after my father's death, we sold our house in Newburgh, New York, and moved to a tiny apartment in the South Bronx, the run-down neighborhood of garages where *Fort Apache* was

filmed. From that dead-end place my mother sent me away to school, urging me on, never letting me quit.

"Don't forget your name," she would tell me. "*Ferro* means iron. You can bend it, but you can't break it. Go on."

I wanted to pay public tribute to my mother, to give her recognition for all she had done for me. That was why I had kept her name professionally after I got married, to honor her. She had fought for our future against so many odds after my father was gone. . . .

My mother taught me by word and example how important it was—for men *and* women—to be self-sufficient. When as a young girl, I begged her to show me how to crochet beads onto dresses, which was how she supported us, she deliberately gave me the hardest bead to try because she knew I'd fail—I did—and be forced to realize how much an education mattered.

I owed my mother so much, not only for her material support, but for the values she had instilled in me: hard work, perseverance, resourcefulness, and a family that comes through for each other.

Mother Teresa

●━━●━━●━━●━━●━━●

On Helping the Poor

The founder of the Society of the Missionaries of Charity, Mother Teresa (born Agnes Gonxha Bojaxhiu in Albania), worked for nearly fifty years to bring hope and dignity to the poor and dying in her adopted country, India, as well as more than twenty-five other nations. She served as a teacher then principal at a Calcutta convent school, and took her final vows in 1937. After eleven years Teresa left the convent to work alone in Calcutta's horrific slums—securing foods, medicine, and funds for the abandoned children she had taken under her wing. In 1957 she began work with lepers and those stricken by natural disasters worldwide.

For her remarkable achievements Mother Teresa was awarded the Pope John XXIII Peace Prize in 1971 and the Nobel Peace Prize in 1979. In *Life in the Spirit* she offered this admonition:

The "shut-ins," the unwanted, the unloved, the alcoholics, the dying destitutes, the abandoned and the lonely, the outcasts and the untouchables, the leprosy sufferers—all those who are a burden to human society—who have lost all hope and faith in life—who have forgotten how to smile—who have lost the sensibility of the warm hand-touch of love and friendship—they look to us for comfort. If we turn our back on them, we turn it on Christ, and at the hour of our death we shall be judged if we have recognized Christ in them, and on what we have done for and to them. There will only be two ways, "come" or "go."

Therefore, I appeal to every one of you—poor and rich, young and old—to give your own hands to serve Christ in his poor and your hearts to love him in them. They may be far or near, materially poor or spiritually poor, hungry for love and friendship, ignorant of the riches of the love of God for them, homeless for want of a home made of love in your heart; and since love begins at home maybe Christ is hungry, naked, sick or homeless in your own heart, in your family, in your neighbors, in the country you live in, in the world.

Ida Chagall and her son Marc

━━━━━━

On Honoring Your Mother

Marc Chagall is ranked among the twentieth century's greatest painters. Associated with the cubist and surrealist movements, his colorful paintings of figures serenely floating over village and urban landscapes are now known the world over. Chagall was born into a deeply religious family in the Jewish townlet of Vitebsk, Russia. In 1910 he moved to Paris, where he first began to paint in a unique style that incorporated religious symbols and childhood memories into the sensual colors and structures of French art of the time.

Over a sixty-year career in the media of lithography, oil paint, theatrical set-and-costume production, ceiling and mural art, and stained glass Chagall never ceased drawing inspiration from his early years in the religiously imbued milieu of prerevolutionary rural Russia. In his evocative, poetic memoir, *My Life,* the famous painter nostalgically wrote:

I see her managing the household, ordering my father about,
always building little dream
houses, setting up a grocery store,
supplying it with a whole wag-
onload of merchandise, without·
money, on credit. With what
words, by what means can I show
her smiling, seated for hours at a
time in front of the door or at the
table, waiting for some neighbor or
others to whom, in her distress, she
may unburden herself?

At night when the shop was
closed and all of us [eight] children
were home, Papa dozed off to sleep at the table, the lamp rested
and the chairs grew bored; out-of-doors we couldn't tell where
the sky was, where Nature had fled; not that we were silent, but
simply that everything was quiescent. Mama sat in front of the
tall stove, one hand on the table, the other on her stomach.

Her head rose to a point at the top where her hair was held in
place by a pin.

She tapped one finger on the table that was covered with an
oilcloth, tapped several times and that meant:

"Everyone is asleep! What children I have! I have no one to talk to!"

She loved to talk. She fashioned words and presented them so well that her listener would smile in embarrassment.

Like a queen, erect, motionless, her pointed coiffure in place, she asked questions through closed lips that scarcely moved. But there was no one to answer her. At a distance, I was the only one to follow her.

"My son," she said, "talk to me."

I am a little boy and Mama is a queen. What shall I say?

She is angry, her finger taps the table repeatedly.

And the house is enveloped in quiet sadness.

So many years have gone by since she died!

Where are you now, dear little mother? In heaven, on earth? I am here, far from you. . . .

Can my words distill for you a little sweetness, tender and caressing?

Grace Hemingway and her son Ernest

On Calling for Maturity

Ernest Hemingway produced such classic twentieth-century novels as *A Farewell to Arms, The Sun Also Rises,* and *For Whom the Bell Tolls.* He developed the plain, forceful writing style that became his hallmark while working as a journalist for the *Kansas City Star;* later he served as a Red Cross volunteer during World War I.

Hemingway grew up in a middle-class family in Oak Park, Illinois. By adolescence he had developed a wild streak that especially upset his mother, Grace. After disappearing one night with a young teenage girl, Ernest received from Grace this powerful admonition:

> For three years, since you decided, at the age of eighteen years, that you did not need any further advice or guidance from your parents, I have tried to keep silence and let you work out your own salvation; by that I mean, your own philosophy of life—your code of ethics in dealing with men, women, and chil-

dren. Now, at the age of twenty-one, and being, according to some of your best friends and well-wishers, so sadly in need of good guidance, I shall brave your anger, and speak this once more to you.

A mother's love seems to me like a bank. Each child that is born to her, enters the world with a large and prosperous bank account, seemingly inexhaustible. The mother is practically a body slave to his every whim.

Thinks the mother, "some day he will be a comfort to me and return all I am doing to him," and she is content.

Then, up to adolescence, while the bank is heavily drawn on, for love and sympathy, championship in time of trouble or injustice, developing the young body and mind and soul—there are a few deposits of pennies, some thoughtfulness and "thank yous."

But now, adolescence is past—full manhood is here. The bank is still paying out love. . . . The account needs some deposits, by this time, some good sized ones in the way of gratitude and appreciation, interest in Mother's ideas and affairs. . . .

Unless you, my son Ernest, come to yourself, cease your lazy loafing and pleasure seeking—borrowing with no thought of returning—[or] there is nothing before you but bankruptcy. You have over drawn.

This world is crying out for men, real men, with brawn and muscle, moral as well as physical—men whose mothers can look up to them, instead of hanging their heads in shame at having borne them.

You are born of [those] who would scorn to accept anything from anybody without rendering a just equivalent, men who were clean-mouthed, chivalrous to all women, grateful and generous. You were named after two of the finest and noblest gentlemen I have ever known. See to it that you do not disgrace their memories.

When you have changed your ideas and aims in life, you will find your mother waiting to welcome you, whether it is in this world or the next—loving you and longing for your love.

Anne Sexton and her daughter Linda Grey

●━●━●━●━●

On Mother's Love

Born in Newton, Massachusetts, Anne (neé Harvey) Sexton was a Pulitzer Prize–winning poet whose writing was richly autobiographical. After working as a Boston fashion model she turned her full attention after World War II to poetry. Her acclaimed books include *To Bedlam and Part Way Back, Live or Die,* and *The Awful Rowing Toward God*.

Anne suffered from severe depression through much of her adult life and committed suicide at the height of her career. In April 1969 Sexton, at age forty, sent this heartfelt letter to her teenage daughter, Linda Grey, who later became her literary executor:

> I am in the middle of a flight to St. Louis to give a reading. I was reading a *New Yorker* story that made me think of my mother and all alone in the seat I whispered to her, "I know, Mother, I know." And I thought of you—someday flying some-

where all alone and me dead perhaps and you wishing to speak to me.

And I want to speak back. (Linda, maybe, it won't be flying, maybe it will be at your own kitchen table drinking tea some afternoon when you are 40. *Anytime*.)—I want to say back

1. I love you.
2. You *never* let me down.
3. I know I was there once. I *too* was 40 and with a dead mother who I needed still.

This is my message to the 40-year-old Linda. No matter what happens you were always my bobolink, my special Linda. Life is not easy. It is awfully lonely. *I* know that. Now you too know it—wherever you are, Linda, talking to me. But I've had a good life—I wrote unhappy—but I lived to the hilt. . . .

Be your own woman. Belong to those you love. Talk to my poems, and talk to your heart—I'm in both if you need me. I lied, Linda. I did love my mother and she loved me. She never held me, but I miss her, so that I have to deny I ever loved her—or she me. Silly Anne! So there!

Louivery Valentine Bell Abernathy
and her son Ralph

●━━●━●━●━━●

On Learning Kindness

Born in rural Alabama, Ralph Abernathy grew up in the racially charged climate of America's Deep South. At an early age he became attracted to the ministry for its humanitarian ideals and, in the 1950s, became a civil rights organizer and a leading confidant of Dr. Martin Luther King Jr. In 1961 Abernathy was appointed pastor of the West Hunter Street Baptist Church in Atlanta, Georgia, a position he maintained throughout his decades of civil rights activism. In 1968 he became Dr. King's chosen successor as head of the Southern Christian Leadership Council, but resigned leadership to run unsuccessfully for Andrew Young's congressional seat nearly a decade later.

Abernathy has in recent years focused mainly on issues of world peace. In his autobiography, *And the Walls Came Tumbling Down,* he reminisced:

I learned about strength, independence, and moral earnestness from my father, while my mother taught me kindness, love, and gentility. . . .

Like every younger child in a large family, I lived with hand-me-downs; I wore them and played with them. But when I went to school I wanted my own books. . . . Books were special to me, and my mother understood how I felt.

My father, on the other hand, was more pragmatic. He had housed, fed, and clothed ten of us, with two more coming up, and he saw no reason why he should have to buy more books. . . .

I tried to protest, but he simply didn't want to listen. There were other needs, other priorities. He was immovable and my eyes filled with tears.

Then I noticed my mother watching me with anguish on her face; and I was amazed to see her dabbing her eyes with her apron. She was crying because of me! I believe it was the first time in my life that I understood what love really meant, that capacity to feel the suffering of others as if it were your own. I was stunned with the sheer beauty of it, and a little frightened as well.

The next day, when I didn't have the right books, I was scolded by the teacher. I assured her that I would have the books by the next day, though my heart was in despair, because I knew my father all too well. However, when I came in the front door after school I saw them piled in a neat stack on the dining room table: all the books I needed, their jackets untorn and unwrinkled, their pages still white and unsoiled.

I knew immediately who was responsible, and I went into the kitchen to hug my mother. Later, when my father came in from the fields, I thanked him as well, but he merely nodded his head and brushed the matter aside. That afternoon, I understood a little more about the world in which I lived than I had that morning.

Jane Austen

●●●●●●

On Making the Right Romantic Choice

Jane Austen is widely considered the first great female novelist. The celebrated early-nineteenth-century author of such enduring works as *Pride and Prejudice, Emma,* and *Sense and Sensibility* was born into affluence and well educated for a woman of her time. Her themes were friendship, love, and the complexities of human affection. Austen never married, but frequently offered guidance to her nieces about affairs of the heart.

In November 1814, for instance, Austen offered this bracing advice to her lovelorn niece Fanny Knight:

> With all my heart, I wish I had cautioned you on that point when you first spoke to me; but though I did not think you then so much in love as you thought yourself, I did not consider you as being attached in a degree—quite sufficient for happiness—as I had no doubt it would increase with opportunity.

Oh! Dear Fanny! Your mistake has been one that thousands of women fall into. He was the *first* young man who attached himself to you. That was the charm, and most powerful it is. Among the multitudes, however, that make the same mistake with yourself, there can be few indeed who have so little reason to regret it.

His character and *his* attachment leave you nothing to be ashamed of. You certainly have encouraged him to such a point as to make him feel almost secure of you—you have no inclination for any other person. His situation in life, family, friends, above all his character—his uncommonly amiable mind, strict principles, just notions, good habits—all that you know so well how to value.... Everything of this nature pleads his cause most strongly.

[But] now, my dear Fanny, having written so much on one side of the question, I shall turn around and entreat you not to commit yourself farther, and not to think of accepting him unless you really do like him. Anything is to be preferred or endured rather than marrying without affection.

And if his deficiencies of manner strike you more than all his good qualities, if you continue to think strongly of them, give him up at once. Things are now in such a state that you must resolve upon one or the other: either to allow him to go on as he has done, or whenever you are together behave with a coldness which may convince him that he has been deceiving himself.

I have no doubt of his suffering a good deal for a time when he feels that he must give you up; but it is no creed of mine, as you must be well aware, that such sorts of disappointments kill anybody.

Mary Ruth Joyner and her daughter Jackie

●━━━━━━

On Heartbreak

Jackie Joyner-Kersee's athletic accomplishments include winning six Olympic medals (three of them gold), holding the current world record in the heptathlon (the women's version of the male decathlon) and the former world record in the long jump, and becoming an All-American basketball player.

Named for Jacqueline Kennedy, Joyner-Kersee grew up in poverty-stricken East St. Louis in a house "little more than wallpaper and sticks." Her parents were poor teenagers when they married but were determined to help their obviously talented daughter make a success of herself. At eighteen Jackie first gained national recognition in track and field.

Mary Ruth died of meningitis when Jackie was only twenty but had a vital influence on her outlook. In her autobiography, *A Kind of Grace,* the renowned athlete recalled:

When I turned sixteen, I fell for a boy on the basketball team. . . . I liked him because we had a common interest in athletics. My mother grew to like him because he was courteous and obeyed her rule that I'd be home by 10:00 P.M. after our dates. She called him a "gentleman."

But as his graduation approached in the spring, he wanted to start a sexual relationship, which I promptly reported to Momma.

"No, no, no," she said, vigorously shaking her head. "We are not making any babies in this house. If he wants sex, he can get it from someone else. You have too much to do in life."

I was head over heels for this guy. Still I wasn't ready for anything serious. He said he wanted to date other girls, which I didn't like, but felt powerless to prevent. Several months later, I heard that the girl he was seeing was pregnant. That night, I sat in my bedroom and cried. Although we'd broken up, his actions felt like a betrayal. Momma came into my room and sat beside me. I told her what happened as she wiped away my tears. "I know it hurts now," she said in a soft voice. "But the pain will go away and you'll see you made the right decision."

Nancy Edison and her son Thomas

━━━━━━

On Respecting Your Child's Uniqueness

Thomas Edison is regarded as the greatest inventor in history. He created such products as the electric lightbulb and phonograph and improved many others, including the telephone, typewriter, electric generator, and electric-powered train. The youngest of seven children born to Nancy and Samuel Edison, Thomas moved at age seven from rural Ohio to Port Huron, Michigan, where his father established a grain and lumber business. As biographer Neil Baldwin recounted in *Edison: Inventing the Century:*

> For a short time, Thomas also attended a one-room public school in Port Huron, with forty pupils ranging in age from five to twenty-one. With frequent colds, respiratory illnesses, and a bout of scarlet fever after the family moved to Port Huron, Thomas was not a well child.

Seeing that Thomas would draw and doodle in his notebook instead of repeating rote lessons, the headmaster—a "Mr. Crawford"—began to ridicule and cuff Thomas in front of his peers. "One day," Edison recalled with bitterness decades later, "I heard the teacher tell the visiting school inspector that I was addled and it would not be worthwhile to keep [me] in school any longer. I was so hurt by this last straw that I burst out crying and went home and told my mother about it.

"Mother love was aroused, mother pride wounded to the quick," Edison continued. Nancy angrily confronted the teacher and told him that he didn't know what he was talking about, that Thomas had more intelligence than he did. Thereupon, Nancy summarily pulled Thomas out of school and began educating the lad herself. As one Edison biographer noted, "She was determined that no formalism would cramp his style, no fetters hobble the free rein, the full sweep of his imagination." . . .

"My mother was the making of me," Edison declared. "She was so true, so sure of me; and I felt I had someone to live for, someone I must not disappoint."

Ernestine Ross and her daughter Diana

●●●●●●

On Sticking Up for Oneself

Diana Ross, a superstar in today's entertainment world, grew up in lower-middle-class 1950s Detroit. Showing early talent, she became lead singer for the female trio known as the Supremes and by her early twenties one of Motown Records' most successful performers. Diana went solo in 1969 and immediately gained new hits with "Someday, We'll Be Together," "Reach Out and Touch Somebody's Hand," and "Ain't No Mountain High Enough." As an actress, her popular movies have included *Lady Sings the Blues* (in which she portrayed singer Billie Holiday) and *Mahogany*. Through live and televised concerts, Diana Ross has retained an enthusiastic following.

In a memoir titled *Secrets of a Sparrow* she recalled this key childhood lesson from her mother:

> One day when I was eight years old, I came home from school in tears. My face was red, and I was terribly beat up. I finally

told Mama that a kid had slapped me in my face. At her past advice, I had walked away.

She stroked my burning cheek. "What did they call you?" she wanted to know.

"They called me 'nigger,' Mama."

Mama's face went cold, and she was really mad. "Don't you ever let anybody hit you in your face and call you a nigger. Yes, you hear me. I mean for you to fight, fight for all you've got. You know, I have never told you to fight before, but I want you to fight for your dear life. Never let anyone make you feel bad about who you are."

One week later, Mama was wiping blood from my nose and washing my bruised face. I had been in a fight, and I couldn't say that I had won. I was ashamed, angry, and confused all at the same time. . . .

It had happened in school. Everything felt dusty and dirty that afternoon. Some kids were picking on me and had called me a name, a bad name, and then they giggled and ran away. I knew that they were trying to make me feel bad about myself, but I didn't. I just felt angry, and I had hauled off and swung at them. They had hit me back twice and scratched my face before they took off running and laughing.

I picked up my schoolbooks and started walking. By the time I reached home, I had made a decision. From now on, I would fight back and just as Mama said, I would win. I had to. No more bloody noses. I had decided this but not because of what Mama said. I made the decision for myself this time. I was never going to let anybody put me down again. It was important for me to be strong and to fight back.

That was a turning point.

Jane Clemens and her son Samuel
(Mark Twain)

●●●●●●●

On Teaching Compassion for All Creatures

Mark Twain, the pen name of Missouri-born Samuel Clemens, is one of America's most intriguing literary figures. In such late-nineteenth-century novels as *The Adventures of Huckleberry Finn, The Prince and the Pauper,* and *A Connecticut Yankee in King Arthur's Court,* Twain combined homespun humor with sharp criticism about the injustices of his time.

Throughout Twain's influential career he showed sensitivity to the suffering of others in all walks of of life. In his famous *Autobiography,* the novelist warmly recalled his mother:

> One day in St. Louis, she walked out into the street and greatly surprised a burly cartman who was beating his horse with the butt of a heavy whip. For she took the whip away from him and

then made such a persuasive appeal in behalf of the ignorantly offending horse, that he was tripped into saying he was to blame; and also into volunteering a promise, which, of course, he couldn't keep, for he was not built that way—a promise he would never abuse a horse again.

That sort of interference on behalf of abused animals was a common thing with her all her life; and her manner must have been without offense and her good intent transparent, for she always carried her point and also won the courtesy and the friendly applause of the adversary.

Mata Amritanandamayi ("The Mother")

•••••••

On the Value of Cooperation

Whereas most major religions have been founded and led by men, Hinduism has produced occasional women who have established ashrams and initiated spiritual movements. One of the most intriguing of such women gurus is Mata Amritanandamayi. Born in poverty, in 1953, in a tiny village in the state of Kerala in West India, she has developed an international reputation as a spiritual master. For the past decade, Mata has made annual tours of European and North American cities—and to her admirers is now known as the Mother for her boundless compassion.

In 1993 Mata was selected at the Chicago Parliament of the World's Religions as one of the three presidents of the Hindu faith. Her inspirational address included these remarks:

> Religions should help people cultivate a strong desire to seek
> eternal life with a firm foundation of love and peace. . . . Mutual

love and cooperation between religions should be of primary importance in the world. Let love, peace, cooperation, and non-violence be the beacons that light the way into the Twenty-First Century.

Today, there are thousands who are ready to die for their religion, but none who are willing to live by its principles. People do not realize that religion is something to be lived. They forget that it has to be applied and practiced in our day-to-day lives. . . .

When we truly imbibe the spirit of religion, the sorrow and suffering of others becomes our own. Compassion arises, and we are able to sympathize with the pain and suffering of others. Only through the experience of oneness with the Self can we feel real compassion and concern.

Gladys Sara Remen and her daughter
Rachel Naomi

•••••••

On Loving-kindness

Rachel Naomi Remen, M.D., is a pioneer trainer of physicians in relationship-centered care. A former member of the Stanford School of Medicine faculty, she currently teaches family and community medicine at the University of California in San Francisco. For the past twenty years, Dr. Remen has specialized in mind-body medicine, with a particular interest in cancer treatment. In her book *Kitchen Table Wisdom: Stories That Heal,* Remen recollected:

> My given name is Rachel. I was named after my mother's mother. For the first fifty years of my life, I was called by another name, Naomi, which is my middle name.
> When I was in my middle forties, my mother, who was at that time almost eighty-five, elected to have coronary bypass surgery. The surgery was extremely difficult and only partly successful.

When [my mother] finally regained consciousness, she was profoundly disoriented and often did not know who I, her only child, was. The nurses were reassuring. . . . Nevertheless, I was concerned. Not only did Mom not know me, but she was hallucinating, seeing things crawl on her bed and feeling water run down her back.

Although she did not seem to know my name, she spoke to me often and at length, mostly of the past, about her own mother who died before I was born and who was regarded as a saint by all who knew her. She spoke of the many acts of loving-kindness which her mother had done without even realizing she was being kind: the shelter offered to those who had none, the encouragement and financial support which helped others, often strangers, to win their dreams. She spoke of her mother's humility and great learning and of the poverty and difficulty of life in Russia which she remembered as a child. She recalled the abuses and hatreds the family experienced to which many others had responded with anger and her mother only with compassion.

I remember one visit shortly before she left the intensive care unit. I greeted her asking if she knew who I was. "Yes," she said with warmth, "you are my beloved child." Comforted, I turned to sit on the only chair in her room but she stopped me. "Don't sit there." Doubtfully I looked at the chair again. "But why not?"

"[My mother] Rachel is there," she said. I turned back to my mother. It was obvious that she saw quite clearly something I could not see.... My mother began to tell her mother Rachel about my childhood and her pride in the person I had become. Her experience of Rachel's presence was so convincing that I found myself wondering why I could not see her. It was more than a little unnerving. And very moving. Periodically, she would appear to listen and then she would tell me of my grandmother's reactions to what she had told her.... She explained to my grandmother why she had given me her name, her hope for my kindness of heart, and apologized for my father who had insisted on calling me by my middle name, which had come from his side of the family.

Exhausted by all this conversation, my mother lay back on her pillows and closed her eyes briefly. When she opened them again, she smiled at me and the empty chair. "I'm so glad you are both here now," she said. "One of you will take me home." Then she closed her eyes again and drifted off to sleep. It was my grandmother who took her home.

This experience, disturbing as it was for me at the time, seemed deeply comforting to my mother and became something I revisited again and again after she died. I had survived many years of chronic illness and physical limitation. I had been one of the few women in my class at medical school in the fifties, one of the few women on the faculty at Stanford medical school in the sixties. I was expert at dealing with limitations and challenges of various sorts [but] I had not succeeded through loving-kindness. Over a period of time, I came to realize that despite my success, I had perhaps lost something of importance. When I turned fifty, I began asking people to call me Rachel, my real name.

Credits

"Dora Birnbaum and her son George Burns" reprinted by permission of The Putnam Publishing Group from *100 Years, 100 Stories* by George Burns. Copyright © 1996 by the Estate of George Burns.

"Adelle Maxwell and her grandson Bill Gates" excerpted from *Gates* by Stephen Manes and Paul Andrews. Copyright © 1993 by Stephen Manes. Used by permission of Doubleday, a division of Bantam Doubleday Dell Publishing Group, Inc.

"Gladys Sara Remen and her daughter Rachel Naomi" reprinted by permission of Riverhead Books, a division of The Putnam Publishing Group from *Kitchen Table Wisdom* by Rachel Naomi Remen, M.D. Copyright © 1996 by Rachel Naomi Remen.

References

Abernathy, Ralph David. *And the Walls Came Tumbling Down: An Auto-biography*. New York: Harper & Collins, 1989.

Abramson, Leslie. *The Defense Is Ready: Life in the Trenches of Criminal Law*. New York: Simon & Schuster, 1995.

Adler, Bill. *The Uncommon Wisdom of Jacqueline Kennedy Onassis*. Secaucus, N.J.: Carol Publishing, 1994.

Anderson, Jervis. *Bayard Rustin: Troubles I've Seen, a Biography*. New York: HarperCollins, 1997.

Anderson, Paul. *Janet Reno: Doing the Right Thing*. New York: Wiley, 1994.

Angelou, Maya. *Wouldn't Take Nothing for My Journey Now*. New York: Random House, 1993.

Asbell, Bernard, ed. *Mother & Daughter: The Letters of Eleanor and Anna Roosevelt*. New York: Coward, McCann, & Geoghegan, 1982.

Ash, Mary Kay. *Mary Kay*. New York: Harper & Row, 1981.

Asimov, Isaac. *In Memory Yet Green: The Autobiography of Isaac Asimov, 1920–1954*. New York: Avon, 1980.

Astor, Brooke. *Footprints: An Autobiography*. Garden City, New York: Doubleday, 1980.

Ball, Lucille. *Love, Lucy*. New York: Putnam's, 1996.

Baraka, Amiri. *The Autobiography of Leroi Jones*. New York: Harper & Row, 1989.

Barr, Roseanne. *Roseanne: My Life as a Woman*. New York: Harper & Row, 1989.

Bateson, Mary Catherine. *With a Daughter's Eye: A Memoir of Margaret Mead and Gregory Bateson*. New York: Morrow, 1984.

Bawden, Nina. *In My Own Time: Almost an Autobiography*. New York: Clarion, 1994.

Bogle, Donald. *Dorothy Dandridge: A Biography*. New York: Amistad, 1997.

Bourke-White, Margaret. *Portrait of Myself*. New York: Simon & Schuster, 1963.

Burns, George. *One Hundred Years, One Hundred Stories*. New York: Putnam's, 1996.

Butterfield, L. H., Marc Friedlander, and Mary Jo Kline. *The Book of Abigail and John: Selected Letters of the Adams Family*. Cambridge, Mass.: Harvard University Press, 1975.

Cahill, Susan, ed. *Wise Women: Over Two Thousand Years of Spiritual Writing by Women*. New York: Norton, 1996.

Caldicott, Helen Broinowski. *A Desperate Passion*. New York: Norton, 1996.

Chagall, Marc. *My Life*. Translated by Elisabeth Abbott. New York: Orion Press, 1960.

Chapman, R. W., ed. *Jane Austen: Letters 1796–1817*. London: Oxford University Press, 1955.

Chaplin, Charles. *My Autobiography*. New York: Simon & Schuster, 1964.

Cheney, Ednah D. *Louisa May Alcott: Her Life, Letters, and Journals*. Boston: Roberts Brothers, 1892.

Christie, Agatha. *An Autobiography*. New York: Dodd, Mead & Company, 1977.

Dallek, Robert. *Lone Star Rising: Lyndon and His Times, 1960–1980*. New York: Oxford University Press, 1991.

Darwin, Charles. *The Correspondence of Charles Darwin, Volume 1: 1821–1836*. Cambridge: Cambridge University Press, 1985.

Davidson, Cathy N., ed. *The Book of Love: Writers and Their Love Letters*. New York: Pocket, 1992.

Easton, Carol. *No Intermission: The Life of Agnes de Mille*. Boston: Little, Brown, 1986.

Edwards, Anne. *Road to Tara: The Life of Margaret Mitchell*. New Haven, Conn.: Ticknor & Fields, 1983.

Eisenhower, Julie Nixon. *Pat Nixon: The Untold Story*. New York: Simon & Schuster, 1986.

Farrell, Suzanne. *Holding on to the Air: An Autobiography*. New York: Summit, 1990.

Ferraro, Geraldine A. *Ferraro: My Story*. New York: Bantam, 1985.

Fitch, Noel Riley. *Appetite for Life: The Biography of Julia Child*. New York: Doubleday, 1997.

Gelderman, Carol. *Mary McCarthy: A Life*. New York: St. Martin's, 1988.

Ginzburg, Louis. *Legends of the Bible*. Philadelphia: Jewish Publication Society, 1975.

Goldberg, Whoopi. *Book*. New York: Morrow, 1997.

Graham, Katherine. *Personal History*. New York: Knopf, 1997.

Hamill, Pete. *A Drinking Life: A Memoir*. Boston: Little, Brown, 1994.

Hart, Kitty Carlisle. *Kitty: An Autobiography*. New York: Doubleday, 1988.

Hasse, John Edward. *Beyond Category: The Life and Genius of Duke Ellington*. New York: Simon & Schuster, 1993.

Holtzman, Elizabeth. *Who Said It Would Be Easy?: One Woman's Life in the Political Arena*. New York: Arcade, 1996.

Jones, Evan. *Epicurean Delight: The Life and Times of James Beard*. New York: Knopf, 1990.

Joyner-Kersee, Jackie. *A Kind of Grace: The Autobiography of the World's Greatest Female Athlete*. New York: Warner, 1997.

Kerouac, Jack. *Selected Letters, 1940–1956*. Edited and with an introduction and commentary by Ann Charters. New York: Viking, 1995.

Kert, Bernice. *Abby Aldrich Rockefeller: The Woman in the Family*. New York: Random House, 1993.

King, Norman. *The Woman in the White House: The Remarkable Story of Hillary Rodham Clinton*. Secaucus, N.J.: Carol Publishing, 1996.

L'Engle, Madeleine. *A Circle of Quiet*. New York: Farrar, Straus & Giroux, 1972.

Levy, Jacques E. *Cesar Chavez: Autobiography of La Causa*. New York: Norton, 1975.

Malhotra, Inder. *Indira Gandhi: A Personal and Political Biography*. Boston: Northeastern University Press, 1989.

Manes, Stephen, and Paul Andrews, eds. *Gates: How Microsoft's Mogul Reinvented an Industry and Made Himself the Richest Man in America*. New York: Doubleday, 1993.

Marler, Regina. *Selected Letters of Vanessa Bell*. New York: Pantheon, 1993.

McBride, Joseph. *Steven Spielberg: A Biography*. New York: Simon & Schuster, 1997.

Meir, Menachem. *My Mother, Golda Meir*. New York: Arbor House, 1983.

Montessori, Maria. *The Absorbent Mind*. Cutchogue, N.Y.: Buccaneer, 1993.

Morton, Andrew. *Diana: Her True Story*. New York: Simon & Schuster, 1997.

Neider, Charles, ed. *The Autobiography of Mark Twain*. New York: Harper & Row, 1939.

Novick, Sheldon M. *Henry James: The Young Master*. New York: Random House, 1996.

O'Brien, Sharon. *Willa Cather: The Emerging Voice*. New York: Oxford University Press, 1987.

Parmet, Herbert S. *George Bush: The Life of a Lone Star Yankee*. New York: Scribner, 1997.

Parton, Dolly. *My Life and Other Unfinished Business*. New York: HarperCollins, 1994.

Phelps, Robert, *Earthly Paradise: Colette's Autobiography Drawn from the Writings of a Lifetime*. Translated by Herma Briffault, Derek Coltman, and others. New York: Farrar, Straus & Giroux, 1966.

Rather, Dan. *I Remember*. Boston: Little, Brown, 1991.

Remen, Rachel Naomi, M.D. *Kitchen Table Wisdom*. New York: Riverhead, 1996.

Reynolds, Michael. *The Young Hemingway*. New York: Blackwell, 1986.

Robinson, Roxana. *Georgia O'Keeffe: A Life*. New York: Harper & Row, 1989.

Ross, Diana. *Secrets of a Sparrow: Memoirs*. New York: Villard, 1993.

Rowan, Carl T. *Breaking Barriers: A Memoir*. Boston: Little, Brown, 1991.

Russell, Bertrand. *The Autobiography of Bertrand Russell, 1872–1914*. Boston: Little, Brown, 1967.

Schikel, Richard. *Clint Eastwood: A Biography*. New York: Knopf, 1996.

Singer, Isaac Bashevis, and Ira Moskowitz. *A Little Boy in Search of God: Mysticism in a Personal Light*. New York: Doubleday, 1976.

Taylor, Ina. *A Woman of Contradictions: The Life of George Eliot*. New York: Morrow, 1989.

Terry, John Skally, ed. *Thomas Wolfe's Letters to His Mother, Julia Elizabeth Wolfe*. New York: Scribner's, 1943.

Thomas, R. David. *Dave's Way: A New Approach to Old-Fashioned Success*. New York: Putnam's, 1991.

Trump, Donald. *The Art of the Deal*. New York: Random House, 1987.

Umansky, Ellen M., and Dianne Ashton, eds. *Four Centuries of Jewish Women's Spirituality: A Sourcebook*. Boston: Beacon, 1992.

Young, Andrew. *An Easy Burden: The Civil Rights Movement and the Transformation of America*. New York: HarperCollins, 1996.

Warloe, Constance, ed. *I've Always Meant to Tell You: Letters to Our Mothers, An Anthology of Contemporary Women Writers*. New York: Pocket, 1997.